PAUL CHAPPELL

OUTSIDERS

15 LEADERS WHO FOLLOWED CHRIST

AND CHANGED THE WORLD

Striving Together
PUBLICATIONS

strivingtogether.com

TIMELINE

John Huss
1369–1415

Peter Waldo
1140–1215

John Wycliffe
1324–1384

1200

1300

Latimer and Ridley
October 16, 1555

John Bunyan
1628–1688

John Newton
1725–1807

1600

1700

William Carey
1761–1834

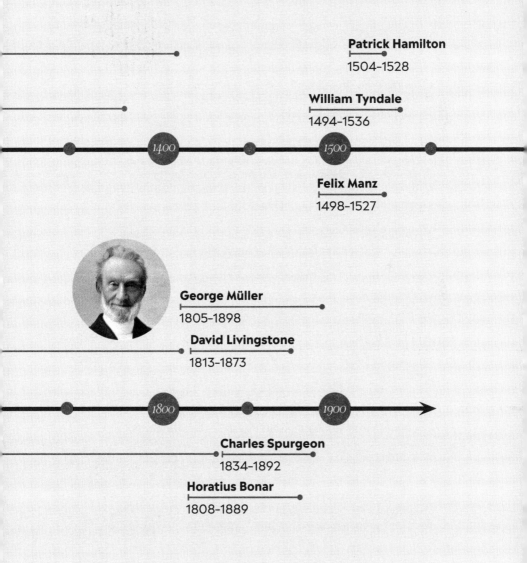

Patrick Hamilton
1504–1528

William Tyndale
1494–1536

1400

1500

Felix Manz
1498–1527

George Müller
1805–1898

David Livingstone
1813–1873

1800

1900

Charles Spurgeon
1834–1892

Horatius Bonar
1808–1889

Copyright © 2019 by Striving Together Publications. All Scripture
quotations are taken from the King James Version.
Special emphasis in verses is added.

First published in 2019 by Striving Together Publications, a ministry
of Lancaster Baptist Church, Lancaster, CA 93535. Striving Together
Publications is committed to providing tried, trusted, and proven
books that will further equip local churches to carry out the Great
Commission. Your comments and suggestions are valued.

All rights reserved. No part of this book may be reproduced, stored
in a retrieval system, or transmitted in any form or by any means—
electronic, mechanical, photocopy, recording, or otherwise—without
written permission of the publisher, except for brief quotations in
printed reviews.

Striving Together Publications
4020 E. Lancaster Blvd.
Lancaster, CA 93535
800.201.7748

The author and publication team have given every effort to give
proper credit to quotes and thoughts that are not original with the
author. It is not our intent to claim originality with any quote or
thought that could not readily be tied to an original source.

Cover and interior design by Andrew Jones
Writing and research assistance by Monica Bass
Additional research assistance by Anna Gregory

ISBN 978-1-59894-401-3
Printed in the United States of America

To the men and women who
dared to believe during the
darkest times in history and
willingly stood outside the
realms of protection and
organized religion to follow
Christ alone.

Wherefore Jesus also, that he might sanctify the people
with his own blood, suffered without the gate. Let us go
forth therefore unto him without the camp, bearing his
reproach.—Hebrews 13:12–13

CONTENTS

ACKNOWLEDGEMENTS

Terrie, thank you for rising early and walking fast through old lanes, churches, and libraries on our quick visits through church history.

Bonnie Ferrso and my office assistants, thank you for coordinating an already-busy schedule to allow me to learn, grow, and explore.

Monica Bass, thank you for incredible help in research, writing, and editing. Thank you for your passion to learn, share, and help to communicate life-changing truth.

INTRODUCTION

J ust outside the old City of London—the one square mile that was settled by the Romans—lies the nonconformists' burial ground known as Bunhill Fields.

Today, London is of course built out miles beyond its City of London center. In fact, it surrounds the tiny, four-acre Bunhill Fields and even uses the little cemetery as a thoroughfare for those wanting to take a shortcut from Bunhill Row to City Road, perhaps to get to the Old Street Underground just down the block.

But if you should linger in the cemetery, you'll find among its headstones such names as Susannah Wesley, John Bunyan, John Rippon (pastor who preceded Charles Spurgeon at the London Baptist Tabernacle), Isaac Watts, and no fewer than seventy nonconformist pastors among its

120,000 graves.[1] Of these, only about 2,000 headstones remain. Many of their names are worn off. Their record is in Heaven.

All of those who are buried in Bunhill Fields had one attribute in common—they were willing to be outsiders. In a period of England's history when uniformity in loyalty, conviction, and thought was required, these brave men and women dissented. They didn't do it merely to be obstinate; they did it because they knew a better way. In most cases, this was a decision borne of love for the Lord and deep-seated biblical convictions.

Jesus Himself was an outsider. Like the corpses of the Old Testament sacrifices that were burned outside the Israelite camp, "Jesus also, that he might sanctify the people with his own blood, suffered without the gate" (Hebrews 13:12).

John Rippon's Grave: During a 116-year span (1720–1836), the church that Charles Spurgeon would later pastor had a succession of two long-serving pastors: Dr. John Gill and Dr. John Rippon. Both are buried in Bunhill Fields.

Bunhill Fields: This four-acre cemetery in the middle of London was used as a nonconformist burial ground from 1665–1854. The name comes from "Bone Hill" in reference to its prior use as a dumping ground for the nearby St. Paul's charnel house.

It is our privilege then as His followers to also "go forth therefore unto him without the camp, bearing his reproach" (Hebrews 13:13).

This, of course, looks different in every culture and every age. None of us are called to be a seventeenth-century nonconformist in England. But all of us are called to follow Christ, knowing that at some level and in some way it will mean ostracism, misunderstanding, and persecution. "Yea, and all that will live godly in Christ Jesus shall suffer persecution" (2 Timothy 3:12).

The church itself is a "called out assembly." This is the meaning of the Greek word Jesus used for *church (ekklesia)* when He told Peter, "Upon this rock I will build my *church*; and the gates of hell shall not prevail against it" (Matthew 16:18).

Indeed, when you look back over history, Christ *has* preserved His church. From the New Testament churches of the first century into even the Dark Ages, we find local churches, often in pockets of persecuted but courageous bodies of believers, who held to the basic truths of New Testament Christianity and refused to join themselves with the corrupted Roman Catholic Church, operating as true, biblical, autonomous churches.

To be sure, the history of these churches is hard to trace, and there isn't a large amount of written history published during their era because they themselves were persecuted, martyred, and their records burned. As Charles Spurgeon so eloquently preached,

> History has hitherto been written by our enemies, who never would have kept a single fact about us upon the record if they could have helped it, and yet it leaks out every now and then that certain poor people called Anabaptists were brought up for condemnation. From the days of Henry II to those of Elizabeth we hear of certain unhappy heretics who were hated of all men for the truth's sake which was in them. We read of poor men and women, with their garments cut short, turned out into the fields to perish in the cold, and anon of others who were burnt at Newington for the crime of Anabaptism. Long before your Protestants were known of, these horrible Anabaptists, as they were unjustly called, were protesting for the "one Lord, one faith, and one baptism." No sooner did the visible church begin to depart from the gospel than these men arose to keep fast by the good old way. . . . At times ill-written history would have us think that they died out, so well had the wolf done his work on the sheep. Yet here we are, blessed and multiplied . . . As I think of your numbers and efforts, I can only say in wonder—what a growth! As I think of the multitudes of our brethren in America, I may well say, What hath God wrought! Our history forbids discouragement.[2]

Indeed, from the Montanists in the second century to the Novatians in the third century to the Donatists in the fourth and the Albigenses throughout the Middle Ages, we find Baptist forefathers who courageously stood for truth and actively proclaimed the Bible. Although some of these groups, or at least some factions of them, misinterpreted and misunderstood significant Bible doctrines, they were stout in their allegiance to Christ and in their operation as called out assemblies of believers.

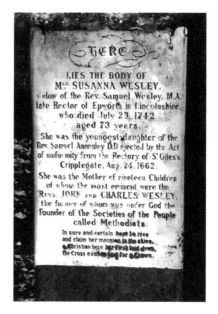

Many Christians today, however, don't want to be called out. Or more specifically, they don't want to *stand* out. They want to blend in with the world around them. Sometimes this is because of a sincere, but unbiblical, belief that

Susannah Wesley's Grave: Susannah Wesley, mother of John and Charles, is buried in Bunhill Fields, along with men such as Isaac Watts and John Bunyan.

they can better reach the world by being like the world. Jesus, who took on Himself human flesh and perfectly adapted to the first-century Jewish culture, was with the world—He was criticized for being friends with society's rejects (Luke 5:30)—but He never blended in with or absorbed the sinful elements of His culture. "For such an high priest became us, who is holy, harmless, undefiled, separate from sinners, and made higher than the heavens" (Hebrews 7:26).

Sometimes Christians today don't want to stand out because of fear. Who wants to be ridiculed, scorned, called a bigot, or ostracized?

The reality is, however, that the men and women who have changed the world have been the men and women the world could not change. A different world cannot be built by indifferent people.

In some ways, of course, it's trendy to be "different," but only the kind of different that everyone would like to be—someone who stands up to the system, who differentiates themselves, who is praised as a *radical*.

But what if being an outsider is less of a cultural ideology and more of a courageous conviction? What if it's not about being heralded as a radical, but about being misunderstood as a bigot? What if it doesn't carry praise at all but brings persecution and even death? Is it still worth it?

I believe the stories in this book answer those questions.

I am often asked why preachers and churches today are shifting from the distinctives of their heritage. I believe at times the reason is a desire for acceptance of the world. Other times it is a quest for significance and popularity. Still other times it may be a lack of theological grounding. But I believe there's more. The shift often stems from a profound lack of knowledge about our heritage and the price that has been paid for the faith we hold.

Over the years, God has given me glimpses into church history as I've had opportunity to visit some of the historic locations connected with great leaders of the past. And in these pages, I'm excited to introduce fifteen such leaders to you.

Most of these were Baptists or forerunners to Baptists. Some were directly connected to the Reformation. A few were evangelicals with broader affiliations. All were men who loved the Lord, were committed to His Word, and lived with biblical convictions that ran contrary to culture.

This book is not an exhaustive study of history—Baptist, Reformation, or otherwise. It also doesn't include nearly as many people as I wish it could, including any of the many women who also fit the outsiders' mold. It is simply a collection of introductions—my attempt to acquaint you with a few of the leaders I've studied.

Also, this book is not exhaustive on any of the lives presented. I hope these chapters will pique your interest to read full-length biographies on the people mentioned in these pages. There are a few here of whom very little has been written and of whom I had to piece together bits of research from various places. I've done my best to provide thorough endnotes. Some of the people mentioned led groups or movements that have compromised greatly since the founder's life (such as the Waldensians and Moravians). I don't think it is necessary to point that out in each chapter and have not done so.

Each chapter in this book provides something of an extended biographical sketch, photos of places relevant to that person's life (many of these are pictures my wife Terrie or I have taken), and a few application thoughts. One of the great benefits in studying the lives of those greatly used by God is seeing through their testimonies a living example of God's Word practiced. I'm always asking myself what biblical truths are evidenced in their lives and how I can apply these in my life. As we conclude each biographical sketch in this book, I'll share some of these practical applications that have impacted me from each life.

Although each chapter stands on its own and you do not need to read in order, since they are arranged in historical order, you may gain shades of historical context by reading in sequence.

New Testament Christianity is a counter-cultural faith. It has always been so, and it always will be. I pray that the stories of these men who lived out their faith as outsiders will encourage you to do the same.

PETER WALDO
(c. 1140–c. 1215)

"Our tears are no longer of water; they are of blood; they do
not merely obscure our sight, they choke our very hearts."

Waldensians of Italy

I t is a curious fact of history that we owe a great deal to people of
whom we know very little.

In Peter Waldo's case, we don't even know if his first name was, in
fact, Peter. And his last name is uncertain as well—Valdès, Vaudès, or
de Vaux are all possibilities. He seems to have been born sometime around
1140 and died sometime between 1205–1218.

But the fact that his life served as a tool to deeply etch the gospel into the
unyielding superstitions and fear of the Dark Ages in countries throughout
Europe is undeniable.

I had come across Peter Waldo's name over the years while studying
church history, usually as a brief introduction to the significance of the
Waldensians as early Baptist forefathers. But it wasn't until several years
ago that Waldo himself first became real to me.

Statue of Peter Waldo in Worms, Germany, memorializing his pre-Reformation gospel ministry.

My wife Terrie and I had spent a few days in Geneva, following the steps of Charles Spurgeon who had preached there as well as the reformers who had been there before him. Realizing that we were only a few hours by train away from the Angrogna Valley, we decided to visit there as well. This is one of the valleys in southeast France and northern Italy where Waldensians had lived for centuries, dating even before the life of Peter Waldo.

As we walked up a stone path to a hidden cave and stooped down to go through the low entrance, we found ourselves inside an area with room for about sixty people. It was in this cave that Waldensians in the twelfth century, during the time of Peter Waldo, met in secrecy from the Roman Catholic authorities to worship, pray, sing, and preach. And it was from this cave, and others like it, that they went out by the hundreds to share the gospel . . . and to be martyred. The price they willingly paid for their faith is convicting to us in twenty-first century comfortable Christianity.

Tucked into the forest of the same valley, we visited a stone hut, built into the contours of the mountainside to conceal it from view, which served as a Waldensian Bible college. In that rough, simple setting, Waldensian young men and women trained for gospel ministry.

This first-hand encounter with the commitment and fortitude of the Waldensians piqued my interest in Peter Waldo. Who was he? And how did his life influence so wide a movement hundreds of years before the Reformation?

• • • • •

Although details of Waldo's early life are blurred to the Dark Ages of history, we find him around 1169 as a wealthy merchant in Lyon, France. He was just under thirty years old, married, and had two daughters. In many ways, his testimony is not unlike Zacchaeus'.

Both Waldo and Zacchaeus were rich through extortion of others. In Waldo's case, it was as a banker who practiced more as a loan shark, becoming wealthy through his neighbors' need. Additionally, he was a cloth merchant with considerable real estate holdings. He was sharp, savvy, and an out-of-the-box thinker.

But God awakened a spiritual hunger within him. An event—of which the details are lost—stirred questions within his heart about death and meeting God. Some say he witnessed a friend suddenly die of a heart attack at a party. Others suggest he heard a troubadour sing about the piety of one of the Catholic saints who died. Whatever sparked his questions, they were there. Waldo couldn't stop wondering if he was ready to meet God.

To find the answers, Waldo searched in two places: a priest and the Bible.

The priest pointed Waldo to Matthew 19:21: "Jesus said unto him, If thou wilt be perfect, go and sell that thou hast, and give to the poor, and thou shalt have treasure in heaven: and come and follow me." Waldo took the verse at direct face value. He told his wife that he was going to sell all he had to follow Christ, but that he would first provide for her and for their daughters. He gave his wife a choice of all his liquid assets or all his real estate. She chose the real estate, and he sold the rest. After securing an education for his daughters, he made restitution to those he had financially wronged and gave the rest of his money to the poor.

Was this decision an attempt to earn salvation? Or was it, like Zacchaeus, a fruit of repentance and the evidence of a life changed by salvation (Luke 19:8–9)? It's hard to say—but I believe it was the second, for a simple reason: At the same time Waldo was seeking answers through the priest, he took a step that was no less creative or direct than Zacchaeus' method of climbing a tree to see Jesus over the crowd. Waldo sought out the Living Word—the Bible itself.

This idea makes a lot of sense to us who have the Bible so easily accessible and with a heritage of those who have pointed to Scripture as the way to God. But for Waldo, this was innovative thinking.

In Waldo's time, it was a settled assumption that the Catholic Church and her leaders had sole access to the Bible—both physically and spiritually. According to the thinking of the Dark Ages, Church leaders were responsible to discern the Bible's meaning, and they interpreted it primarily through the paradigm of Church tradition. Tradition, having been practiced so many years and by those who held such power, was surely infallible. The Church would then relay what God wanted of the people to them—no questions asked. Lay people, of course, could not understand the Bible or be responsible to discern truth from heresy.

But if custom and culture would not philosophically dissuade Waldo, there was the matter of practical impossibility: Waldo couldn't read Latin, at least not well, and the only Bible to which he would have had access was in Latin.

And this is where Waldo made what was to be the most impactful decision of his life: he hired priests to translate the Bible into Franco-

Provençal, the common language of his region. This was a language he *could* read and in which he would soon preach. And this decision opened the door, if only just a crack, letting the light of God's Word shine into the Dark Ages of Europe. Every other great moving of God throughout Europe would have the translation of Scripture at its onset.

If the date of Waldo's salvation is uncertain, the reality of it is not. Soon, he began to preach the blood of Jesus as the complete substitutionary sacrifice for sin. In time, he would also directly preach against works, including the sacraments of the church, as having any part in our salvation.

When I read about Waldo's life and see the similarities between his and Zacchaeus' conversion, I can't help but wonder where Zacchaeus ended up. This I know: both met Jesus, and He transformed their lives.

● ● ● ● ●

Waldo devoured God's Word as a starving man discovering a banquet feast. He memorized all four Gospels and some of the epistles and began preaching on the streets. People listened in amazement as, for the first time, they heard the Bible in their own language. The power of Scripture and the simple message of the gospel drew many to faith in Christ.

In between preaching, Waldo put his faith into practice as he spent his time visiting the poor and outcasts of the town, praying and sharing Scripture with them, and ministering to their needs. He had a living faith that exemplified James 1:27: "Pure religion and undefiled before God and the Father is this, To visit the fatherless and widows in their affliction, and to keep himself unspotted from the world."

Those who came to Christ through Waldo's witness began following his example. Most sold their possessions, gave to the poor, and preached everywhere they went. In fact, generous poverty and Bible preaching became the double-hallmark of Waldo's followers.

John Foxe notes that the poverty of the Waldensians was not merely for the sake of poverty itself, but was the natural result of the persecution that followed wherever they went.[1] Before the persecution picked up, however, Waldo had another motive—itinerant ministry. How could he freely travel to preach if he were burdened down with possessions? His great life's purpose was to preach the gospel, and he followed it passionately, preaching in Lyon and as far as he could in surrounding areas.

Of this period in Waldo's life, Stevan Borbone De Bellavilla, a Catholic leader and Waldo's contemporary, disparagingly wrote, "So he succeeded in gathering together men and women, and teaching them the Gospels induced them to do the same. Though they were poor and illiterate, he sent them to preach through the surrounding villages. They, men and women, silly and illiterate, going here and there through the country, entering into the houses, and preaching in the squares and also in the Churches, induced others to do the same."[2]

And so, through the foolish and weak, "silly and illiterate," God made His gospel known. "For ye see your calling, brethren, how that not many wise men after the flesh, not many mighty, not many noble, are called: But God hath chosen the foolish things of the world to confound the wise; and God hath chosen the weak things of the world to confound the things which are mighty; And base things of the world, and things which are despised, hath God chosen, yea, and things which are not, to bring to nought things that are . . . That, according as it is written, He that glorieth, let him glory in the Lord" (1 Corinthians 1:26–31).

And, as happened from the earliest days of church history recorded in Acts, opposition followed. Waldo's commitment to Christ and determination to preach the gospel would soon take him far beyond Lyon.

Waldensian Cave: Encased in the glass is the Franco-Provençal Bible. This cave is located in the Piedmont Valley and is one in which Waldensians met for church in the twelfth century.

• • • • •

It was initially the practical aspects of the Waldensians' faith, rather than their doctrine, that angered the local priests. That these lay preachers were serving the poor and needy in ways that the clergy had left undone only pointed to the hypocrisy of the priests. Under the pretense of doctrinal differences, the priests complained to the Archbishop of Lyon about these unqualified lay men and women who were going everywhere preaching the Bible from the common language with no doctrinal training.

The result was that Waldo was called before the Archbishop and commanded to cease and desist. His response paralleled another Peter who in Acts 5:29 was similarly forbidden to preach Christ: "Then Peter and the other apostles answered and said, We ought to obey God rather than men."

Waldo's response before the Archbishop reveals both his knowledge of the New Testament (he referenced Acts 5:29 as well as Mark 16:15) and his understanding of and commitment to the Great Commission: "Judge you whether it is lawful before God to obey you rather than God, for we cannot refuse to obey him who hath said, 'Go ye into all the world and preach the Gospel to every creature.'"[3]

Determined to continue preaching and confident that the Archbishop misunderstood, Waldo traveled to Rome and appealed directly to Pope Alexander III in 1179. The Pope was impressed with Waldo's genuine piety and granted a convoluted form of approval. Waldo could continue preaching as long as he had the approval of the local bishops (which he, of course, did not).

In this strained form of freedom, the Waldensians continued to preach, and the local authorities continued to command them to stop. And as the cycle continued, people responded to the message of the gospel by the thousands.

In 1184, however, Pope Lucius III (Alexander III's successor), in a determined effort to stamp out the Waldensians, held a synod in which he excommunicated Waldo and his followers and any who would aid or abet them in their mission.

Lucius' ruling, however, had two unintended consequences.

First, it helped to develop Waldo's doctrinal distinctives. Prior to this time, while he preached salvation by grace, it seems he struggled to separate the Catholic sacraments from faith. The synod's excommunication, however, freed Waldo to study God's Word, not through the lens of Church tradition, trying to reconcile the two, but through the lens of basic, New Testament instruction and practice.

The result was that whereas previously Waldo had seen himself as a reformer—seeking to bring the Church back to a simple and obedient faith—now he recognized that the Catholic Church was not a New Testament church at all and soon preached against all of its core teachings.

In a short time, Waldo and those he trained would set forth articles of faith that directly countered the Catholic Church. Below is a summary of a list provided by John Foxe:

- That Scripture is the final authority in all matters pertaining to salvation.
- That nothing should be added to Scripture by religious systems for salvation.
- That Jesus is the only Mediator and the saints should not be looked at as mediators.
- That there are only two places of eternal destination—Heaven and Hell—and that purgatory does not exist.
- That baptism and the Lord's table are the only ordinances of the New Testament church, and they are not part of salvation.
- That prayers for the dead are anti-biblical.
- That the supremacy of the pope above all churches and above government is usurped. (They went further to say, "The church of Rome is the very Babylon spoken of in the Apocalypse; and the pope is the fountain of all errors, and the very antichrist.")
- That relics, pilgrimages, holy water, and decrees of feasts and fasting and eating restrictions had no place in the church.[4]

Waldo not only preached against these unbiblical doctrines, but he began to plant local churches independent of the Catholic Church.

The second God-ordained consequence of the Waldensians' excommunication was that the persecution which followed drove them across Europe preaching the gospel and planting churches everywhere they went.

I mentioned earlier that the Waldensians actually predate Peter Waldo. (Some historians believe that they are named for the valleys in which they lived rather than after Waldo himself.) It was likely during this time of persecution and scattering that Peter Waldo and the group from Lyon came to be identified with the *Waldensian* title, as they shared the same doctrine.

In fact, the fierce, harsh persecution had the same effect as Saul's persecution of first-century Christians in the New Testament: "...And at that time there was a great persecution against the church which was at Jerusalem; and they were all scattered abroad throughout the regions of Judaea and Samaria" (Acts 8:1). The more severe the persecution, the further the gospel spread.

The Waldensians were so passionate to spread the gospel that they found remarkably creative ways to do it.

Piedmont, Italy, where Waldensian Christians were persecuted in the "Massacre of Piedmont." That Waldo's followers were still preaching the gospel four hundred years after his death is testimony to the power of Scripture and the value of a life given over to Christ.

As I mentioned earlier, their Bible colleges were hidden in the mountains. In these stone huts or caves, *barbas* (the colloquial word for *uncle*, as Waldensian pastors and teachers refused the Catholic title of *Father*) would train young men and women for ministry.

I was humbled as I saw the rough benches around the hewn stone podium where the barba would teach from the center. The eager students were not only risking their lives in attending the school, but they were also literally preparing themselves for martyrdom.

In secrecy, the barbas trained their students to read and write in multiple languages and to rightly divide the doctrines of God's Word. Additionally, they taught enough about medicine or trade to enable them to travel with the disguise of a physician or merchant. When they graduated, they would be traveling evangelists, preaching the gospel message to an unfriendly audience. For many of them, it was not a question of if they would be martyred, but of how much they could accomplish before martyrdom came.

· · · · ·

Waldo himself moved to Dauphine in southeastern France, where he continued to preach. Later, pushed out of Dauphine, he moved to Picardy in northern France. Here his ministry once again swelled with new converts, so that French King Augustus eventually sent an army to brutally silence them. Waldo managed to move next to Bohemia. Once again, the Lord blessed his preaching and church planting ministry. Some historians claim that there were as many as *forty thousand* Waldensian Christians throughout this region as a direct result of Peter Waldo's gospel and church planting ministry.

From around 1205, there is no further definitely recorded history of Peter Waldo, although John Foxe believes that he died as late as 1218. Did he continue church planting and die of a natural cause? Was he martyred in one of the mass executions carried out against the Waldensians?

We don't know. But we do know that the death of Peter Waldo didn't end the persecution of the Waldensians. For the next seven hundred years, they were fiercely and brutally persecuted with a hatred that could only come from Hell itself.

Near where I visited in the Piedmont valleys of Italy, one of the most-remembered of these persecutions occurred in 1655. In January of that year, the Duke of Savoy forced a cruel choice upon the Waldensians of the lower valleys in Italy—either attend Catholic Mass, or move out of the valley within three days. In the dead of winter, some two thousand people journeyed across swollen rivers, snow-buried valleys, and ice-covered mountains with traces of blood marking their trail—all to avoid compromise.

Waldensians in the upper valleys welcomed the refugees and shared their meager provisions freely. But the worst was yet to come.

In April of the same year, the Duke of Savoy sent an army to the upper valleys. Deceived by accounts of Waldensian resistance, he ordered a gruesome slaughter.

Saturday, April 24, 1655, at 4:00 a.m., the signal was given for a general massacre.

The horrors of this massacre are indescribable. Not content to simply kill their victims, the soldiers and monks who accompanied them invented barbaric tortures: Babies and children had their limbs ripped off their bodies by sheer strength. Parents were forced to watch their children tortured to death before they themselves were tortured and killed. Fathers were forced to wear the decapitated heads of their children as the fathers were marched to their death. Some of these Christians were literally plowed into their own fields. Some were flayed or burned alive. Many endured worse. Unburied bodies—dead and alive—covered the ground.

Hundreds of the Waldensians fled for a large cave in the towering Mount Castelluzzo. The murderous soldiers, however, found them there and hurled them down the precipice to their death. This is the reference in Milton's famous sonnet to "the bloody Piedmontese that rolled Mother with infant down the rocks."

Survivors of this massacre were few, but they rallied together and wrote to Christians in Europe for help. Their letters included the heart-rending words, "Our tears are no longer of water; they are of blood; they do not merely obscure our sight, they choke our very hearts."[5]

When Oliver Cromwell heard news of the barbaric massacre, he called for a national day of fasting in England and collected money to send to meet the physical needs of the Waldensians.

The poet John Milton honored the brave, uncompromising courage of the Waldensians with a now-famous sonnet:

"On the Late Massacre in Piedmont"
Avenge, O Lord, thy slaughtered saints, whose bones
Lie scattered on the Alpine mountains cold,
Even them who kept thy truth so pure of old,
When all our fathers worshiped stocks and stones;
Forget not: in thy book record their groans
Who were thy sheep and in their ancient fold
Slain by the bloody Piedmontese that rolled
Mother with infant down the rocks. Their moans
The vales redoubled to the hills, and they
To Heaven. Their martyred blood and ashes sow

O'er all th' Italian fields where still doth sway
The triple tyrant; that from these may grow
A hundredfold, who having learnt thy way
Early may fly the Babylonian woe.

The direct persecution of Waldensians continued into the seventeenth century. In World War II, these who had known persecution took in Jews who were persecuted. During the Nazi occupation of North Italy, Italian Waldensians actively saved Jews, providing hiding places in the same mountain valley where their own ancestors had found refuge in earlier generations.

Although the Waldensian churches today do not believe what they once did, God used this group of people to keep a light burning for Him and for truth throughout Europe during the Dark Ages. At the time of Peter Waldo's death and in the century after, the Waldensians had active local churches throughout France, Italy, Germany, Austria, Bohemia, Moravia, Poland, Spain, and beyond.

And approximately 150 years after Peter Waldo's death in Bohemia, another man was born in the same region who surely heard the gospel through the witness of the Waldensians. Like Peter Waldo, John Huss would carry the light of truth, and he would allow himself to be extinguished for its blaze.

TRUTHS FOR OUTSIDERS

What do we learn from the life of Peter Waldo?

God's Word is powerful. Waldo is credited with providing the Bible to Europe in the first modern language, outside of Latin. And we see, first through Waldo's conversion and then through his ministry, the supremacy of Scripture. It was Scripture itself that revealed to Waldo the truth of the gospel, and it was the translated Scriptures that the Waldensians carried that allowed them to so powerfully share the gospel with others. The spread of the gospel throughout Europe over the next four hundred years always followed the translation and availability of God's Word in vernacular languages. "Is not my word like as a fire? saith the Lord; and like a hammer that breaketh the rock in pieces?" (Jeremiah 23:29).

True riches are eternal. Even if Waldo did originally liquidate his wealth and give it away to earn salvation, he eventually discovered that it was not enough to buy eternal life (Matthew 16:26). But once he knew Christ, he also realized that temporal wealth was empty, outside of using it to meet basic needs, give to others, and further the work of the gospel. Remember that Waldo had keen business acumen, which is how he became wealthy in the first place. But for the remainder of his life, he chose to live unencumbered by wealth.

Although God does not call all Christians to a lifestyle of poverty, He does call all Christians to generously give to His work and to ". . . lay up for yourselves treasures in heaven, where neither moth nor rust doth corrupt, and where thieves do not break through nor steal: For where your treasure is, there will your heart be also" (Matthew 6:20–21).

The spread of the gospel depends on its human proclamation. Waldo could have avoided persecution had he kept his faith to himself. Yet, the spread of the gospel has always depended on the proclamation of the gospel. Paul shared with the Ephesian elders, "And how I kept back nothing that was profitable unto you, but have shewed you, and have taught you publickly, and from house to house" (Acts 20:20).

How did Peter Waldo reach so many people with the gospel? How did Waldensians multiply and spread across Europe even under intense persecution? Because Waldo and Waldensians were preachers. They were bold and unashamed to publicly proclaim the gospel.

Christ will build His church. It's encouraging to remember that the church is indestructible. Jesus told Peter, ". . . upon this rock I will build my church; and the gates of hell shall not prevail against it" (Matthew 16:18). Under the oppressive reign of the very organization that twisted and abused this promise claiming that the pope was the church's rock, the Waldensians flourished in the spread of local churches. They were persecuted and slaughtered, but they only grew.

A single spark of light makes a difference in the dark. It's easy for all of us to question the effectiveness of our lives. Sometimes we see such great spiritual need around us and wonder if we can even make a difference . . . indeed, if we are making a difference. But Waldo's life is witness to the reality, "The darker the night, the brighter the light." Don't let unbelief hinder your effectiveness for Christ. "Let your light so shine . . . That ye may be blameless and harmless, the sons of God, without rebuke, in the midst of a crooked and perverse nation, among whom ye shine as lights in the world" (Matthew 5:16, Philippians 2:15).

2

JOHN WYCLIFFE
(c. 1324–1384)

"Englishmen learn Christ's law best in English. Moses heard
God's law in his own tongue; so did Christ's apostles."

John Wycliffe

On a clear winter's night in the North Riding of Yorkshire, England, where John Wycliffe was born on a humble sheep farm, the morning star can be seen on the horizon more than three hours before dawn. Its bright presence heralds the coming of the rising sun and a new day. The morning star, in fact (which is properly known as the planet Venus), is so bright it can even cast shadows.

Such was the life of John Wycliffe, sometimes referred to today as "the morning star of the Reformation." Born some two hundred years before the Reformation, Wycliffe used his influence to shine light into the spiritual darkness of England during his lifetime, and he left a lasting shadow both through the preachers he trained and, especially, his most-remembered accomplishment—the first full Bible translated into English.

• • • • •

I suppose if those who knew Wycliffe in his early years had known the remarkable ways in which he would impact history, the date of his birth might have been more carefully recorded and remembered. As it is, however, we only know he was born in the mid-1320s in the northern section of Yorkshire, about 250 miles north of London.

In 1346, Wycliffe left Yorkshire for Oxford University, enrolling in Queen's College. His early studies included natural science and mathematics, but he directed his doctorate toward theology. Eventually, he transferred from Queen's College to Merton, where he became a fellow, and finally to Balliol where he was Master of the College.

These were formative years for Wycliffe; and although they were years of comparative solitude, they were also a time of profound significance.

Early in Wycliffe's time at Oxford, the first wave of the Black Plague began spreading through England. Over one third of the nation's population died in its five-month peak in 1349, and before its retreat, it claimed the lives of over half of England. (Between 1347–1351, at least 25 million people died across Europe.) For months, spotted, rotting corpses were visible in fields and known to be in houses where every member of the household had died. This experience left a profound mark on the twenty-five-year-old thoughtful, contemplative Wycliffe. Some biographers trace his conversion to Christ to this time.

Wycliffe was gifted with a brilliant mind and he was an exceptionally deep thinker. This combination shone brightly at Oxford, where he was renowned as a philosopher and lecturer long before he completed his doctorate in 1372. Never a bombastic personality, these quiet years gave him time and space to develop skills in the disciplines of logic and persuasive public speaking.

St. Paul's Cathedral, London: Wycliffe's first trial for heresy was held at St. Paul's Cathedral in London. Due to a petty disagreement among his accusers, the trial turned into a riot and disbanded. After Wycliffe's death, the Catholic Church burned copies of his Bible translation outside the Cathedral by the statue of the Apostle Paul.

More importantly, however, in these years of study and teaching, Wycliffe began to develop a love for God's Word. In a move unusual to his time, Wycliffe began to include in his teaching curriculum extensive lectures on the Bible itself and on individual passages or books of the Bible. Most courses of theology taught only the doctrines of the Church apart from Scripture and with the study of the writings of early Church fathers. Ironically, doctors of theology thought that lecturing on the Bible was simplistic and beneath them. For Wycliffe, however, the more exposure he had to Scripture, the more he loved it. And the more he loved it, the more concerned he became that what he had been taught and was teaching was inaccurate.

Lambeth Tower, London: Wycliffe's second trial was held at Lambeth Palace, the residence of the Archbishop of Canterbury, which is connected to this tower. The Lollards would later be imprisoned in such large numbers in Lambeth Tower that it became known as Lollard's Tower. In the second picture, you can see the inscription on the door reading "Lollard's Tower."

At some point, Wycliffe came to two convictions through his study of Scripture: Salvation is by Jesus alone through faith. And the Bible—not Church tradition—must be the guide for truth and the standard of local church practice. Eventually, Wycliffe would preach and write against the Catholic doctrines and practices of transubstantiation (that the bread and wine of communion became the literal body and blood of Christ and that then receiving that communion is how Christ is literally "received" for salvation), indulgences, and the confessional. And, although he never broke away from the Catholic Church, he did make a clear stand for salvation by faith alone. "Trust wholly in Christ," he wrote, "rely altogether on His sufferings; beware of seeking to be justified in any other way than by His righteousness. Faith in our Lord Jesus Christ is sufficient for salvation.

There must be atonement made for sin according to the righteousness of God. The person to make this atonement must be God and man." In this statement, you hear echoes of 1 Timothy 2:5, "For there is one God, and one mediator between God and men, the man Christ Jesus."

These quiet years of Wycliffe's life also brought to light his extraordinary skill in language. In twelfth century Europe, the vernacular language of a given nation was despised by the academia and high society, with Latin used almost exclusively in scholastic or theological writing, study, and lecture. This was due, in part, to academic snobbery, but perhaps more significantly to the influence of the Catholic Church over higher learning. Another factor that made Latin the language of academia was the variance in vernacular languages from region to region. (Surprisingly enough, Latin was also often used in the political spheres as well.) In any case, Wycliffe not only became adept in using Latin, but he became skillful with it. He grasped its nuances and was fluent, articulate, and persuasive as he used it. Additionally, because of his rural upbringing, he was also fluently articulate in English, which was more than many people in higher learning could claim. Wycliffe's skill in both of these languages would prove extraordinarily beneficial when he began translating the Bible.

•　•　•　•　•

Wycliffe first gained public notoriety in 1366 when the Pope demanded a tax from England. Wycliffe, who was well versed in English law, encouraged Parliament to refuse. From a patriotic standpoint, Wycliffe believed that Rome had no business demanding civil taxes. And from a spiritual standpoint, Wycliffe was becoming increasingly alarmed by the hypocrisy, abuses, and doctrine of the Catholic Church. This event thrust Wycliffe into the public eye and gave him great favor among the English people. In future years, he would become even more beloved for

1382

Wycliffe, translating from the Latin Vulgate, produced the first complete Bible translated for English-speaking people.

1516

Erasmus compiled Greek manuscripts for a complete Greek New Testament. This is known today as the Textus Receptus.

1526

Tyndale translated the New Testament from the Greek. He later began translating the Old Testament.

1535

Myles Coverdale, apparently unbeknown to Tyndale in prison, picked up in Chronicles where Tyndale had left off in the Old Testament and published a complete English Bible.

1537

John Rogers, known by the pseudonym Thomas Matthew, published the second

his consistent preaching and for his personal ministry to the needy. He later wrote, "Visit those who are sick, or who are in trouble, especially those whom God has made needy by age, or by other sickness, as the feeble, the blind, and the lame who are in poverty. These you shall relieve with your goods after your power and after their need, for thus biddeth the Gospel." These words were no empty platitudes; they were borne out of the practice of his pastoral heart.

Wycliffe had been ordained as a priest in 1351. While still spending most of his time at Oxford, he briefly served as the vicar (something like a pastor) in Fylingham. In 1374, a couple of years after receiving his doctorate, Wycliffe moved to Lutterworth, a town about sixty miles north of London. He would preach here until his death ten years later, and it was here that the most fruitful years of Wycliffe's ministry took place.

The first five years of Wycliffe's time in Lutterworth were most significant because of his emphasis on preaching and training other preachers. The first set of men Wycliffe trained were former students from Oxford who had become ordained priests. Eventually, he would train laymen as well, and perhaps it was this training that convinced him of the need to translate the Bible into English. The men he trained became known as Lollards. (The original meaning of the word is lost to history. Some suggest it was a derogatory term that meant "mumblers of prayers." Others believe it meant "wanderers." Both terms are accurate in that these were devout, itinerant preachers.) Because Wycliffe and the Lollards' preaching so relied on Scripture, they were also derisively called "Bible men."

Wycliffe's pastoral training was robust, and his curriculum included teaching on expositional preaching as well as standing in the face of persecution. And the persecution that came would be fierce.

• • • • •

As loved as Wycliffe was by the English people near where he served, he was hated by the Catholic bishops in England and their leaders in Rome. Wycliffe was called to stand trial for his theological views and preaching on three separate occasions. But in every instance, God divinely shielded him from martyrdom, allowing him to start and finish the work for which we remember him today.

complete edition of the Bible in English. This translation is Tyndale's work with revisions on Coverdale's portion. It is the first English translation in which all of the Old Testament is translated from Hebrew.

1539
The Great Bible is published by Myles Coverdale and placed in every church.

1560
The Geneva Bible is translated in Switzerland and distributed in England. It is the first Bible that added numbered verses to the chapters.

1604
King James commissions a new translation of the Bible to provide an official version for the nation. The team of translators relied heavily on Tyndale's translation.

1611
The King James Version is officially published.

Early in 1377, Archbishop Sudbury summoned Wycliffe to answer his critics at St. Paul's Cathedral in London. But before the trial could even commence, disagreement broke out over whether or not Wycliffe should stand or sit for the proceedings. The disagreement broke into riot, and the trial disbanded.

Later in the same year, Pope Gregory XI issued five bulls (public decrees) condemning Wycliffe's views. By this time, however, Wycliffe did not believe in the authority of the pope as a biblical position at all. Thus, he simply disregarded the orders and continued his work. Providentially, this was just months before the Great Schism occurred, in which two men claimed to be the legitimate pope. (Eventually, there would be three claimants to the title, something we'll come back to in our next chapter.) This papal schism made it understandably difficult for Rome to follow

Balliol College: John Wycliffe was for some years Master of Balliol College in Oxford University. It would be just outside of Balliol that Latimer and Ridley would be burned at the stake some 250 years later.

through on prosecuting Wycliffe. It also made Wycliffe's political views for England to exercise greater sovereignty from Rome more popular in his homeland. Consequently, he was only called to Lambeth Palace to answer the charges the following year.

Lambeth Palace was, and remains today, the residence of the Archbishop of London. At Wycliffe's 1378 trial, the hall was filled to capacity, primarily with commoners who were sympathetic to Wycliffe. Once again, before the trial proceeded very far, it was stopped. This time it was interrupted by a messenger sent by Joan of Kent, the mother of the king, who requested that no judgment be brought before Wycliffe at this time. God had again shielded the preacher who would soon take up the task of translating His Word.

In 1382, without Wycliffe even present, a newly-installed Archbishop Courtenay assembled a synod to condemn Wycliffe's writings. They found Wycliffe's teaching guilty of heresy on twenty-six counts and received authorization from the King to arrest and imprison anyone who preached these doctrines.

Since Wycliffe's pastoral training had been underway for quite some time, this ruling was directly aimed at the Lollards. These men would suffer tremendously—during Wycliffe's time and in the three centuries following—for their faith and their courageous preaching.

It was humbling for me to stand by Lambeth Tower, next to Lambeth Palace, where the Lollards were imprisoned and held to await trial in such great numbers that it became known as Lollard's Tower. From Lambeth Tower, you can look across the River Thames to Parliament Square. It's amazing to realize that you are surrounded by busy city activity filled with people who are either ignorant of or indifferent to the sacrifices made there. This whole area, in fact, holds grievous history of Lollard suffering and martyrdom. In nearby Lambeth Fields, hundreds of Christians were slaughtered for their faith. One hundred twenty miles north in Norwich, an area right outside the city wall would become known as Lollard's Pit because of the many Lollards burned there for their faith. Across England, the Lollards were imprisoned, tortured, and burned by the hundreds.

Wycliffe's final trial was in 1383 when he was brought to Oxford to be judged by bishops and doctors. Still the brilliant, logical orator, Wycliffe's arguments left his judges with no response. As they debated among themselves, he simply walked away and returned to continue his duties at his church in Lutterworth.

• • • • •

Wycliffe began his most significant life work—as well as his occupation most egregious to the Catholic Church—in 1379 when he began translating the Bible into English.

Wycliffe translated from the Bible he had available to him at the time— the Latin Vulgate, translated in the fifth century by Jerome, a Catholic priest. Fluent in Latin, Wycliffe translated to make the Scripture available to the common English people. Among these were the Lollard preachers who, armed with Scripture, would canvass England with the gospel.

Wycliffe finished a first draft—the very first complete Bible for English-speaking people—in 1382. Wycliffe himself began revising his first translation immediately after it was finished. He would not complete this revision in his lifetime, but his assistant, John Purvey, completed it about four years after Wycliffe's death.

For sake of comparison, below is Genesis 1:3 in both the early and the later Wycliffe translations, followed by the Tyndale translation and then the King James. (I'm leaving the spelling original to illustrate how greatly English has changed from Middle English, when Wycliffe translated.)

- **Early Wycliffe:** And God seide, Be maad liȝt; and maad is liȝt.

- **Later Wycliffe:** And God seide, Liȝt be maad; and liȝt was maadj.

- **Tyndale:** Than God sayd: let there be lyghte and there was lyghte.

- **King James:** And God said, Let there be light: and there was light.

When Martin Luther translated the Bible into German and Tyndale into English in the 1520s, they had the distribution aid of a printing press—a luxury which Wycliffe did not have. In Wycliffe's day, it required *ten months* of full-time writing to produce one full copy of the Bible. The fact that for many years, Lollards and other "Wycliffites" were burned at the stake with their copies of the Bible, and *still* nearly 150 of these hand-copied manuscripts survived, is an amazing testimony to how many copies must have been proliferated and how readily they must have been received.

One hundred years after Wycliffe's Bible, Tyndale would translate the Bible, not from a Catholic Latin version, but from the Greek and Hebrew languages in which the Bible was originally penned. Mainly because of his source material, Tyndale's translation was more accurate. Because of the shift in language, it was also more usable. Some 150 years after Tyndale, King James would authorize a translation in which a team of scholars participated and cross checked one another's work. Their work, which built on Tyndale's (90 percent of the New Testament is identical to Tydnale's), was also more accurate, correcting errors the single translator had missed. Even so, it is Wycliffe to whom every English-speaking lover of God's Word owes a debt of gratitude for breaking the barriers to the entire Bible being translated into English.

• • • • •

Wycliffe died on New Year's Eve in 1384, just days after suffering a stroke. But his legacy lived on.

The Lollards were an active force for the gospel for another three hundred years. John Huss was greatly influenced by Wycliffe.

Wycliffe was so despised by the Roman Catholic Church that more than forty years after his death, his body was dug up, his bones burnt, and his ashes tossed into the river. Although this action was meant as a desecration to Wycliffe's remains and a warning to others, the spread of his ashes served as a picture of his influence which had already spread. With the Bible translated into the language of the people, it was too late to undo the knowledge of the truth.

As I stood by the side of the River Swift in England where Wycliffe's ashes were tossed, I comprehended the truth of historian Thomas Fuller's observation: "They burnt his bones to ashes and cast them into Swift, a neighboring brook running hardby. Thus this brook hath conveyed his ashes into Avon, Avon into Severn, Severn into the narrow seas, they into the main ocean. And thus the ashes of Wycliffe are the emblem of his doctrine, which now is dispersed the world over."[1]

John Foxe added, "Though they dug up his body, burnt his bones, and drowned his ashes, yet the Word of God and the truth of his doctrine, with the fruit and success thereof, they could not burn; which yet to this day . . . doth remain."[2]

As we'll see in coming chapters, the work of Wycliffe touched almost every other aspect of the Reformation—through the translated Bible and the Lollard preachers. With the arrival of Scripture in English, the morning star had risen over Europe, and there was no turning back the clock.

TRUTHS FOR OUTSIDERS

What do we learn from the life of John Wycliffe?

Despise not the day of small beginnings. Who would have guessed that the young boy growing up on a sheep farm would reshape Europe with the gospel? Who knew that the thoughtful, quiet scholar at Oxford would give England the Bible? "For who hath despised the day of small things? for they shall rejoice, and shall see . . . " (Zechariah 4:10). No person or place is too small or insignificant to be used by God. Serve Him faithfully where you are.

Keep learning and growing. It was Wycliffe's developed skills, particularly in logic and in Latin, that allowed him to have such an impact in preaching and translating the Bible. Has God given you an aptitude or gift? Develop it, and put it to use.

Purposefully invest in others. Wycliffe could have spent his life simply preaching and pastoring, but his decision to train gospel preachers had an impact hundreds of years after his death. The impact of the Lollards' witness, preaching, and careful copying and carrying of the Scriptures for the next two hundred years is impossible to overestimate.

God has given us the responsibility to pass on to others the truths that have been handed to us, and to do it in such a way that they are able to likewise hand those truths to others: "And the things that thou hast heard of me among many witnesses, the same commit thou to faithful men, who shall be able to teach others also" (2 Timothy 2:2). This never happens by accident. It requires intentional investments of time, prayer, and teaching.

Love and study God's Word. World-changing outsiders aren't wild-eyed renegades. They are people who are grounded in God's Word and clearly see its eternal truths. Wycliffe taught and translated the Bible because he loved the Bible. It was his study of Scripture that led him to salvation, and it was his love of Scripture that compelled him to make it available to others.

In Isaiah 55:10–11, God tells Isaiah, who was similar to Wycliffe in that he did not see a national turning to God during his faithful ministry, that God's Word always makes a difference. Sometimes it is like fresh rain and bears immediate results, and sometimes it is like snow and doesn't bear results until a later season when it melts: "For as the rain cometh down, and the snow from heaven, and returneth not thither, but watereth the earth, and maketh it bring forth and bud, that it may give seed to the sower, and bread to the eater: So shall my word be that goeth forth out of my mouth: it shall not return unto me void, but it shall accomplish that which I please, and it shall prosper in the thing whereto I sent it." Wycliffe sent out God's Word, and in two hundred years, it would dramatically change Europe as the gospel spread.

3

JOHN HUSS
(c. 1369–1415)

"What I taught with my lips I now seal with my blood."

John Huss

Every year on July 6, the people of the Czech Republic celebrate "Jan Hus Day." Jan Hus, or as we usually spell his name in the States, John Huss, was born in Bohemia (modern Czech Republic) in 1369. He was born to a poor family in a village named Hussenitz, which means "goose town," and from which he later took his own last name, Hus ("goose").

Raised in the Church of Rome, Huss learned that salvation is obtained through works, that prayer should be made to statues and saints, and that Church tradition, rather than Scripture, was the supreme authority for faith and practice.

As a young man, Huss enrolled in the University of Prague with the intention of becoming a priest. By his own account, his plans for the priesthood were motivated more from wanting to better his station in life rather than because of a love for God or desire to serve Him.

At the university, Huss studied theology and earned bachelor's and master's degrees as well as a doctorate. He became an ordained priest in 1400. But most importantly, it was there at the university where Huss discovered the truth of the gospel.

•   •   •   •   •

Huss' first exposure to the gospel was through Wycliffe's writings, which he encountered through an unusual sequence of events and providential intersection of lives. A man by the name of Jerome of Prague studied at universities throughout Europe, including in Prague, Paris, Heidelberg, Cologne, and Oxford. While at Oxford, Jerome learned English and discovered Wycliffe's writings. He began translating them into Czech, and they made their way back to the University of Prague, where Huss began reading them.

Huss was drawn to the logic and zeal of Wycliffe's defense of Scripture as the authority for doctrine, and these writings prompted Huss to begin studying the Bible with interest. Eventually, Huss would embrace many of Wycliffe's teachings. Throughout his life, however, it remained important to him that it was not so much Wycliffe's teaching, but his own convictions based on his understanding of God's Word, which he taught and preached.

In 1402, Huss was appointed the rector of the University of Prague as well as the preacher for the newly-built Bethlehem Chapel in the city. The name "chapel" is misleading, for this building was the most popular church in one of Europe's largest cities, seating three thousand people. And when the newly-appointed Huss began preaching in Czech rather than Latin and passionately and clearly explained the doctrine of salvation by grace as well as the truths that the Bible must be our authority for doctrine and that Christ is the head of the church, well—the chapel filled to capacity twice a day.

Huss' bold preaching didn't escape the notice of the authorities. In 1403, the Church officially banned many works of Wycliffe. But that did not stop Huss, who began translating and distributing some of Wycliffe's writings which Jerome had not.

When Jerome later arrived in Prague, he was pleased to find many discussing Wycliffe and, especially, the truths of which Wycliffe had written. It was not hard for him to recognize that John Huss (whose sermons, according to the Roman Catholic Church, were full of "anabaptistical errors"[1]) was the center of this discussion and activity. Soon a deep friendship, centered on a mutual love for the gospel and Scripture, ignited.

In direct opposition to orders from Rome, Huss continued preaching against the errant doctrine of the Catholic Church. He was able to do this for a few reasons: First, he had the sympathy of King Wenceslaus IV. Second, the people of Prague loved Huss. And third, there was a growing sense of independence among the Czech people, who were not eager to have their beloved preacher silenced from faraway Rome.

As a counter-move, the pope issued an order that all of Wycliffe's books were to be burned and the preaching of his doctrine be stopped. Huss and anyone subscribing to his doctrine were excommunicated. To ensure compliance, the pope went one step further and put the city of Prague under interdict, disallowing the entire city from taking the sacraments. That was the trump card, and in 1412, Huss quietly left the city.

Huss returned to his hometown of Hussenitz where he continued to preach and began writing. Over the next two years, he wrote prolifically and trained young preachers to continue preaching the gospel. He knew his time was short.

It is remarkable that Peter Waldo, John Wycliffe, and John Huss—all serving in different countries and during different time spans—each

Huss' Martyrdom: A 1415 painting of John Huss' martyrdom. Notice the paper "crown" on his head. This had demons drawn on it and Latin writing which translates, "A ringleader of heretics."

gave the prime years of their lives to training gospel preachers. By following the biblical pattern of 2 Timothy 2:2, their work continued through the labors of those they trained: "And the things that thou hast heard of me among many witnesses, the same commit thou to faithful men, who shall be able to teach others also."

Furthermore, the ministry of these three groups—the Waldensians, Lollards, and Hussites—sowed the gospel seed up and down Europe hundreds of years before the Reformation, and these men watered it with their own blood as they willingly gave themselves as martyrs.

• • • • •

In late 1414, Huss was called to stand trial at the Council of Constance. When he declined to go, knowing that he would surely be convicted of heresy for his biblical preaching and writings, Emperor Sigismund promised him safe conduct to and from the trial. "Even if he had killed my own brother . . . he must be safe while he is at Constance," he guaranteed.[2] The fact that Huss wrote out his will before leaving seems to indicate he didn't take the emperor's promise seriously.

Huss arrived in Constance on November 3, 1414. He was imprisoned on November 28. And what of Emperor Sigismund's promise? Well, he couldn't be expected to be held to promises he had made to a heretic, now could he? Thus, before Huss' trial, his fate was already sealed. He was imprisoned as a heretic and would be tried as an already-convicted heretic.

For over five months, Huss sat in the underground dungeon of a monastery. In a cold, dark cell next to the sewer, always hungry and mostly in poor health, Huss privately and faithfully continued to live out his commitment to Christ. Who can know what thoughts, concerns, and fears entered those hours of solitary confinement or what prayers were whispered. Surely he was grateful for the Bible passages he had committed to memory, which gave him fresh courage for what was ahead.

• • • • •

To understand the Council of Constance, its power, and its purpose, you have to know a significant, but often overlooked, bit of Roman Catholic history. At the time this council convened (indeed, the reason for it being called), there were three men who claimed to be the pope. After Urban VI was selected Pope in 1378, the cardinals who elected him soon regretted their decision. In protest against him, some of them elected a rival pope, Clement VII. Naturally, both men wanted to retain the papacy, and turmoil ensued.

In 1409, the cardinals tried to resolve the problem they had created by declaring both popes heretical and appointing a third pope, Alexander V (later succeeded by John XXIII). Not surprisingly, all three popes excommunicated each other as they sought to establish themselves as the pope.

But this wasn't just about who was in charge of the Catholic Church. Because of the complex way in which the Catholic Church and the various nations throughout Europe were intertwined in their political power and spiritual authority, the insecure position of a Church with three popes was making room for nations to assert their individual power, which would effectively limit the power of the Church.

And this was a problem that the Council of Constance determined to solve, which they ultimately did in November of 1417 by carefully deposing the current popes and electing Martin V.

Understanding this background and the primary purpose for this council makes their secondary purpose even more intriguing—to stop the spread of Wycliffe and Huss' "heresy." The fact that the council cared almost as much about the preaching and writing of these two men shows just how effective their ministry was and is a testimony to God's faithfulness in the spread of the gospel. God had so blessed the faithful witness of Wycliffe and Huss and the men they trained to spread the gospel that these relatively insignificant men were a threat to the entire Roman Catholic Church.

In the opening session, John Wycliffe was named, and by the eighth session, on May 4, 1415, he was condemned. As mentioned in the previous chapter, Wycliffe had died forty years earlier, so the council was not able to condemn him to be burned at the stake, as they would Huss two months later. They did, however, have Wycliffe's body exhumed, burned to ashes, and thrown into the Rhine River.

When Huss stood at trial, his accusers recited their grievances against him. In his response, he explained that he appealed to Christ who was a Judge higher than the pope (a point that also pointed to the assumed authority of this council). As he spoke, they mocked him and condemned him to be burned.

Before Huss was led to the stake, the council made him don the garments of a priest, which they then removed one at a time as they mocked and degraded him. But that wasn't enough. Huss, like other priests in his day, had a *tonsure*—the crown of his head kept shaved to signify devotion to God. After removing all of the priestly garments, the council discussed how to remove the tonsure—and in the end, *sliced it off with a pair of shears.* On top of his profusely bleeding head, they placed a paper hat on which they had drawn demons and written the words, "A ringleader of heretics."

Pulpit in a Hussite Church: Through the efforts of the gospel preachers John Huss trained, Hussite churches were planted all throughout what is today the Czech Republic. These churches endured fierce persecution.

Huss responded, "For my sake, my Lord Jesus Christ wore a crown of thorns, so for His sake why should I not wear this light crown, even though it is a shameful thing."[3]

Huss was led to the stake where he was chained to it. Again he spoke of Christ and expressed willingness to follow Him: "My Lord Jesus Christ was bound with a harder chain than this one for my sake, so why should I be ashamed of this rusty chain?"[4]

They piled sticks around him and made an effort to get him to recant. "No," he responded, "I never preached any doctrine that was evil, and what I taught with my lips I now seal with my blood."[5]

That last phrase, *What I taught with my lips I now seal with my blood,* not only echoes through the corridors of history as an oft-remembered quote, but it accurately describes the courage and conviction with which followers of Christ have given their lives for Him through the ages.

As the executioner lit the fire, Huss began singing, which he continued to do until the flames took his life.

Although Huss' life was cut short, he had no regrets. He could say with Paul, "For I am now ready to be offered, and the time of my departure is at hand. I have fought a good fight, I have finished my course, I have kept the faith: Henceforth there is laid up for me a crown of righteousness, which the Lord, the righteous judge, shall give me at that day: and not to me only, but unto all them also that love his appearing" (2 Timothy 4:6–8).

• • • • •

And what of Jerome of Prague? His amazing story, not told often enough, is one of loyal friendship to Huss and great commitment to Christ.

When Jerome heard that Huss had been arrested, he immediately made his way to Constance, hoping to be of assistance. By the time he reached the city, however, it was obvious to all that, although Huss had not yet stood trial, he was already condemned. Friends explained the situation to Jerome and urged him to leave. Not only would there be no realistic help in court by Jerome's testimony, but Huss was prohibited from receiving any visitors, so Jerome could not even cheer him by his presence.

Grieved, Jerome began the journey back to Prague. But in Northern Germany he was found, arrested, and brought back to Constance. Like Huss, he was imprisoned and condemned as a heretic. He was burned at the stake on May 30, 1416, almost a year after Huss.

When the executioner walked behind Jerome to light the fire, Jerome said, "Come here in front of me and light the fire where I can see it. If I were afraid of it, I would not have come to this place."[6]

• • • • •

The news of Huss' death spread quickly to Bohemia where he was loved and revered. Indeed, martyring Huss was a poor decision by the Council of Constance as it proved to fan the flames of the gospel in Bohemia. The preachers Huss had trained continued preaching, leading people to Christ, discipling them, and training them to do the same. What became known as the Hussite movement spread rapidly, including to neighboring Moravia (also part of the Czech Republic today).

The Bohemian Brethren and Moravian Brethren persisted in the spread of the gospel through severe persecution. Today, they are remembered as some of the earliest gospel missionaries. Four centuries after Huss' death, they were not only still in existence but were leaders in one of the greatest missionary movements of history under the leadership of Count Zinzendorf. From Moravia, they took the gospel to places around the world including the Caribbean, North and South America, the Arctic, Africa, and the Far East.

If John Huss could have known what flames the Holy Spirit would kindle through his martyrdom, he would not have done anything differently. Indeed, his own counsel written before his death was clear: "Therefore, faithful Christian, seek the truth, listen to the truth, learn the truth, love the truth, tell the truth, defend the truth even to death."[7]

TRUTHS FOR OUTSIDERS

What do we learn from the life of John Huss?

We need to develop strong Bible convictions. What impelled John Huss and thousands of other martyrs to sacrifice their lives rather than to recant their faith? What empowered their resolve to make a difference that resonates even today? The answer to both questions is that they had biblical convictions embedded within their souls.

We live in a culture that downplays the importance and relevancy of biblical convictions. But convictions are essential. Jude 20 states, "But ye, beloved, building up yourselves on your most holy faith, praying in the Holy Ghost." God challenges us to stand strong in our distinct biblical position—our "most holy faith." When you are convinced of the truth, you are willing to give everything for it.

Be faithful to your friends. We can only imagine the encouragement it must have been to Huss if he heard that Jerome had tried to come help him. There was obviously a closeness between these two men as, in Bohemia, they strengthened one another in the Lord. Jerome's loyalty in going to Constance is a picture of Proverbs 17:17: "A friend loveth at all times, and a brother is born for adversity."

God's Word sustains, even in death. Sometimes as we read of martyrs, we wonder if we would have the strength to be tortured without denying Christ. But I think we forget or underestimate the power of God's grace and His Word. Although John Huss' last statement to the world was, "What I taught with my lips I now seal with my blood," his actual last words were the Psalms he was reciting as the flames engulfed him. Like Jesus, he found strength through the Psalms in the hour of death.

Lengthen your legacy by purposefully teaching others. The Apostle Paul knew that the "glorious gospel of the blessed God . . . was committed to my trust" (1 Timothy 1:11), so he intentionally discipled others to be able to carry on the message and work of the gospel even after his death. The training of others was so essential to the spread of the gospel during the Dark Ages that it bears repeating.

If you want to make a difference for Christ that lasts beyond your own life, give yourself to discipling others. This may not be as a pastor or a person in full-time ministry. But whether you are a parent, teacher, coach, neighbor, friend, church member, or any other person whose life intersects with others, there are people around you in whom you could invest for Christ.

FELIX MANZ
(c. 1498–1527)

"And thus I close with this: I will firmly adhere to Christ and
trust in him who is acquainted with all my needs and can
deliver me out of it. Amen."

Felix Manz

Which biblical doctrines are worth one's life? Is it *only*
salvation by grace alone? Or is it also the very nature of
what constitutes a New Testament church?

Also, how far should one go in accepting Scripture
alone as the authority for faith and practice? And should that answer
change if the state is willing to accept partial adherence to Scripture but
forbids full obedience?

These are the questions the Anabaptist martyrs answered for us during
the Reformation.

We know that many of the reformers risked, and often gave, their lives
to reclaim the gospel from centuries of obfuscation in the Roman Catholic
Church. But what we sometimes forget is that even the reformers, for

the most part, retained a strong allegiance to the idea of a state church. They wanted the church to be correct in its doctrine, but they struggled to grasp the concept of a free church with Christ—not the government—as its functioning head. Rather than a pure New Testament church, they envisioned a reformed Catholic Church. And when it became apparent to them that the Catholic Church was unwilling to reform, they developed churches with different doctrine but similar polity to the Catholic Church. Because of this, they also struggled to allow freedom of religion and felt threatened by those who taught differently than they did, especially the Anabaptists (a group we'll describe in this chapter).

Consequently, some of the reformers actually persecuted and even executed Anabaptists. Felix Manz was the first of these Anabaptist martyrs to die at the hands of one of the reformers.

• • • • •

I have stood several times on the bank of the Limmat River in Zürich, Switzerland, the place where Felix Manz was drowned for believing, teaching, and practicing believer's baptism. And each time I do, I'm overwhelmed with gratitude for Manz's courage, witness, and gospel ministry.

Manz was born in Zürich, Switzerland, the illegitimate son of a Catholic priest. (Births such as his, in fact, represent one of the many issues that troubled the reformers and spurred them to want to see reform in the church. Although priests were prohibited from marriage, their children were many.)

We know little about Manz's early life and education, but he seems to have been well educated in Hebrew, Greek, and Latin. And in 1522, we find him studying in these very languages with Ulrich Zwingli and a group of other young men.

You may remember Zwingli from history as the leader of the Swiss Reformation. He was a brilliant scholar and a committed reformer. From coming to Zürich in 1519 as a Catholic priest who had already understood the gospel and was determined to preach it, to leading the city to break with the Catholic Church in 1520, Zwingli was a deliberate, causative leader who endeared a whole city, including its city council, to himself and brought about a peaceful reform.

Part of Zwingli's approach had been to attract younger men to his ideas of reform by inviting them to study Greek, Hebrew, and Latin with him. Through this, he introduced them to the Greek New Testament (which Erasmus had just made available a few years prior) and thus to the truths of the gospel. Conrad Grebel was one of the early participants in the group, and Felix Manz followed. In 1522, both men understood the gospel and came to Christ through Zwingli's teaching, and especially through the New Testament to which he had pointed them.

Also through Zwingli's teaching, both men came to the conviction that Scripture should be the final authority for faith and practice. For this reason, they eagerly supported Zwingli in his work of reform.

River Limmat: The River Limmat begins from Lake Zürich in the southern end of the city and flows northwest through the city and through what is known as the Limmat Valley. In this photo, Ulrich Zwingli's church can be seen in the background.

Over the next year, however, Grebel and Manz found it increasingly difficult to trust Zwingli. Although he claimed that Scripture was the final authority, he deferred in practice to the Zürich city council in doctrinal matters, eventually contradicting himself on such issues as the mass and the use of images in the church in order to stay in line with the wishes of the city council. Privately, he shared scriptural views, but publicly, he acquiesced to the wishes of the council, seemingly believing that in time, they would come around if he would just take it slow.

After a publicly-held disputation, set forth by the city council in which Zwingli completely capitulated his previously-stated positions to the direction of the council, Grebel and Manz knew they could no longer work with Zwingli.

Over the following year, as Grebel, Manz, and a few others continued to study the Bible and to preach the gospel throughout the Zürich region, they found themselves studying the question of baptism and the larger question of *what actually is a church?*

●　●　●　●　●

It's difficult for us today to understand why the issue of believer's baptism would be significant enough to have people executed for teaching it. Much of the answer lies in the issue of a state church.

As mentioned earlier, the reformers (Zwingli and Calvin included) did not necessarily have a problem with there being a state church; they simply had a problem with that church teaching Catholic doctrine as a means for salvation. They just wanted to *reform* the system that was already in place. And a key component of keeping this system running was infant baptism.

Grebel and Manz, however, were coming to the scriptural understanding that, for all its centuries of practice, infant baptism was not once to be found in Scripture. Furthermore, they realized that believer's baptism—

baptism by immersion after a profession of faith—was both taught and practiced throughout the New Testament. Finally, they realized that a New Testament church was not comprised simply of a group of citizens who happened to be born in the same town; rather, it was comprised of saved and baptized people who gathered in shared allegiance to Christ and doctrinal agreement.

While this may seem like a simple doctrinal distinction between infant and believer's baptism to those of us who have long enjoyed freedom of religion, in sixteenth-century Europe, the distinction was significant.

Infant baptism was a way of making all of the citizens of a geographic location part of the same church, and that church was inseparably tied to the state. The marriage of state and church created complex civil issues that would be undermined by people individually interpreting Scripture and following their conscience.

Those who believed in infant baptism called those who held the opposing position *Anabaptists*. *Ana* is the Latin word for *re*, thus the literal definition is "re-baptizers." Because practically everyone in Europe at this time in history had been baptized as infants, Anabaptists were accused of rebaptizing. Those who believed in this practice, however, preferred the term *Baptists*. They argued that they were not rebaptizing, but only scripturally baptizing. After all, infant baptism was not baptism at all but merely "dipping in a Romish bath."[1] (This is one of the many reasons it grieves me when those in ministry decide to follow a blending in philosophy, leaving off the name *Baptist* lest there be a stigma associated with it. Those who bore the name centuries ago did it at peril of their own lives because they so valued the biblical doctrine it represented.)

When you think about it, *not* practicing believer's baptism put Zwingli in an odd position. First, he had proclaimed that Scripture alone should be the authority for faith and practice, and he had earlier preached against infant baptism. (Later, as this came into conflict with the city council, he said he had been mistaken.) Second, while he preached salvation by grace alone, infant baptism put the church in Zürich in a practical position in which there were adult members who had been baptized as infants but never made a personal profession of faith.

And herein lies one of the dangers of a state church. It cannot be a true, New Testament local church. And this is why believer's baptism became so important to Grebel and Manz. Over the next several months, these two men as well as several others who shared their commitment to Scripture

Plaque by the Limmat River: This plaque is in a wall near the Limmat River in Zürich. Translated into English, it reads, "Here in the middle of the Limmat, Felix Manz and five other Anabaptists were drowned during the Reformation period between 1527 and 1532. The last Anabaptist to be drowned was Hans Landis, executed in 1614."

began to meet. They continued studying Scripture privately, preaching publicly, and raising the issue of baptism and the New Testament church.

• • • • •

On January 17, 1525, the city council decided to settle the matter with a formal hearing. Manz and Grebel were among those who presented the "radical" viewpoint of believer's baptism, while Zwingli and others argued for infant baptism.

The council came down strongly on the side of infant baptism, issuing a two-fold ordinance that should serve to hinder the Baptists. First, they declared that all parents in Zürich *must* baptize their children within one week of birth or be banished from the city. Second, they declared that to practice believer's baptism was to choose imprisonment.

Manz, Grebel, George Blauock, and nearly a dozen others chose the latter.

On the night of January 21, 1525, four days after the city council's decree, these men went to Felix Manz's home, prayed for courage and faithfulness to Christ, and were baptized. First, Grebel baptized Blauock, and then Blauock baptized the rest.

Thus, on one cold January night, the first Baptist church in Zürich was formed.

• • • • •

The local church, as a body of saved, baptized believers, isn't an obscure doctrine in the New Testament. The book of Acts tells us about the first church in Jerusalem and how the first-century Christians then established churches in other cities as the gospel spread. The next nine books in our New Testament are epistles written to local churches. The three epistles following these are written to local church leaders. Thus, the majority of the New Testament epistles specifically deal with the organization and operation of the local church.

Ephesians 5:25 tells us that "Christ also loved the church, and gave himself for it." And Acts 20:28 reminds us that the flock, the local church, is something that Christ "purchased with his own blood."

Thus, Manz, Grebel, and Blauock were not foolishly grandstanding. They were simply placing the same value on the church as Christ did.

The following months were difficult for the small group in Zürich. Grebel and Manz went house to house sharing the gospel. They baptized new believers, and they administered the Lord's Table. Many were added to their church over the next few months.

Grebel soon went to other cities, continuing his preaching ministry and starting new churches with newly-baptized believers. Manz continued in Zürich.

By October of that year, Manz, Grebel, and Blauock were arrested and imprisoned together. Soon, many others were added to their number in prison. One historian said that during those winter months "the Zürich tower rang with the hymns and prayers of the indomitable prisoners."[2]

On March 7, 1526, the men were brought to trial and condemned to life imprisonment on bread and water. The same day, the city council decreed, "Whoever hereafter baptizes someone will be apprehended by our Lords and, according to this present decree, be drowned without mercy."[3]

Two weeks later, Manz, Grebel, Blauock, and twenty-one others were helped by an unknown benefactor to escape from prison. They went right back to their work, spreading out across Switzerland with the gospel and planting new churches.

Later that summer, Grebel died of the plague. Blauock would preach for three more years, the first of those often with Manz, carrying the gospel across Switzerland and later into Austria and Italy before being burned at the stake in northern Italy in 1529.

Back to Manz: the ten months following his prison escape are hard to trace, except by where he was imprisoned and the churches he started. Two weeks after his first escape, Manz baptized a woman in Embrach, about twelve miles from Zürich. Two months later, Manz and Grebel were again imprisoned. Apparently they escaped or were released, for a few months later, Manz was again arrested. This time he was in St. Gall, some fifty miles from Zürich. Once again, he was released. (One historian pointed out, "Hardly a prison in the vicinity of Manz's labors escaped being honored by his presence.")[4]

Finally, in December of 1526, Manz, along with Blauock, was arrested in a forest and imprisoned a final time. On January 5, 1527, Manz was sentenced to death by drowning for the crime of baptizing and through baptism assembling a church: "Because . . . he had become involved in Anabaptism, . . . because he confessed having said that he wanted to gather those who wanted to accept Christ and follow Him, and unite himself with them through baptism, . . . so that he and his followers separated themselves from the Christian church . . . ."[5]

• • • • •

On the same afternoon that Manz was sentenced, he was taken to the River Lammat for his execution. From prison to the river, he witnessed to all he could of saving faith in Christ alone, and he praised God that he, a sinner, was forgiven by Christ and assured a home in Heaven. His mother and brother were among those on the shore, and as he was put into the fishing boat to be taken out, they called out, encouraging him to be faithful to Christ.

The executioner tied Manz's hands behind his knees and pushed a pole between so he could not free himself. As he was tied, he offered up his last words, "Into thy hands, O God, I commend my spirit."[6] He was rowed out to the middle of the river and pushed overboard.

He was not yet thirty years old. Yet, in less than one year's time, he had been instrumental in starting the first Anabaptist church in Zürich as well as preaching and planting Anabaptist churches throughout Switzerland. Manz and thousands of Anabaptist martyrs freely gave their lives for Christ.

$$\bullet \quad \bullet \quad \bullet \quad \bullet \quad \bullet$$

One of the most remarkable traits of the Anabaptists, besides their commitment to Scripture as a source of doctrine and practice, was their understanding of religious liberty, even against the backdrop of the Middle Ages in Europe.

For instance, consider the contrast between Zwingli and the Anabaptists. Some say that Zwingli was among those on the river bank the day Manz was executed and that he sarcastically commented, "If he wishes to go under the water, let him go under."[7] In other words, if he insists on baptism, let him be drowned. Whether or not this is true, the reformers never seemed to understand the scriptural position of the Anabaptists. Zwingli and Calvin, in particular, were harsh in their treatment of them—even to the point of persecution.

Yet, less than two years before Manz's death, during the initial imprisonment of Grebel, Manz, and Blauock, Grebel had written a manuscript on baptism and offered it up as a basis to dispute Zwingli on the subject. Furthermore, he offered that if Zwingli won the debate that he (Grebel) would be willing to be burned. Whereas, he said, that if he (Grebel) were to win the debate, he would not demand that Zwingli should be burned.[8] His offer was denied.

One author wrote that there were more Anabaptist martyrs after the Reformation than there were Christians who died in the early persecutions of Rome.[9] And yet, we recognize that while it is true that the reformers had their faults and blind spots, they did not all share in the persecution of Baptists. There were, indeed, many non-Anabaptist reformers who also offered up their lives for the gospel. Although the treatment of Anabaptists is a blight on the names of some of the reformers, we are grateful that God used even these men to break the political power of the Roman Catholic Church. This break eventually brought Europe out of the Dark Ages and would eventually pave the way for true religious liberty for all—even for Anabaptists and other nonconformists.

TRUTHS FOR OUTSIDERS

What do we learn from the life of Felix Manz?

All of Scripture is vital to our faith. There is a thought process in contemporary Christianity that advocates setting aside doctrinal distinctives in matters not essential to the gospel to work better with other Christians. While there is great merit in loving and appreciating all gospel-preaching Christians (Philippians 1:18), we cannot set aside the doctrinal truths essential to the local church. Remember that when Paul bid his farewell to the elders of the church at Ephesus, he reminded them of the importance of the whole of Scripture and admonished them to feed the flock of God, the local church, with what they had been taught: "For I have not shunned to declare unto you all the counsel of God. Take heed therefore unto yourselves, and to all the flock, over the which the Holy Ghost hath made you overseers, to feed the church of God, which he hath purchased with his own blood" (Acts 20:27–28).

For Manz it wasn't enough that Zwingli preached the gospel. Manz believed it was important to practice New Testament polity for a local church. He could have set his convictions aside as non-essential, preferring instead to work with Zwingli for the cause of the gospel. Instead, he believed biblical doctrine—even in non-gospel matters—was worth his life.

Love the local church. While Zwingli believed that the best way to propagate the gospel was through the establishment of government-sanctioned religion, Manz correctly saw the local church as the God-ordained vehicle for the Great Commission. Thus, Manz made the local church his center of gospel ministry.

As a Baptist, I believe in the separation of church and state (Matthew 22:21; Acts 5:29–31; Romans 13:1–4), but this belief should be combined with a commitment to actively share the gospel through the ministries of a local church.

Sharing the gospel is as worthy of martyrdom as believing the gospel. Manz didn't only believe the gospel and hold to Baptist doctrine under the threat of death. He didn't only choose to practice the New Testament pattern of believer's baptism under threat of death. He actively preached the gospel and biblical doctrine under threat of death. Manz was a soulwinning church planter under the shadow of prison and sword.

Trust God with the results of your Spirit-filled efforts. I think what most surprised me as I studied Manz's life is how short and effective his ministry was. From the night he was baptized to the day he was drowned was less than two years. Yet in those two years, he and others effectively planted Anabaptist churches throughout Switzerland. He could have compromised his convictions in hope of lengthening his ministry. But instead, he chose to be faithful to God's Word, and God supernaturally extended the reach of his ministry.

God does not call us to success, but He does call us to faithfulness. "Let a man so account of us, as of the ministers of Christ, and stewards of the mysteries of God. Moreover it is required in stewards, that a man be found faithful" (1 Corinthians 4:1–2). Or, more precisely, in faithfulness, we find our success.

WILLIAM TYNDALE
(c. 1494–1536)

"I defy the Pope, and all his laws; and if God spares my life,
ere many years, I will cause the boy that driveth the plow to
know more of the Scriptures than thou dost!"

William Tyndale

I t is difficult, perhaps impossible, to fully imagine what our lives would be like today without the Bible in our language. And it's even more difficult to imagine a culture that prohibits such a translation.

But this is exactly the world into which William Tyndale was born in 1494.

In England, Henry VII was on the throne, soon to be replaced by his son, Henry VIII. The Catholic Church was at the height of its power. Reformers such as John Wycliffe and John Huss had made some headway, but the European world was still entrenched in superstition, spiritual darkness, and great abuses of power.

To keep its control, the Church still maintained a ban on Bible translation into any modern language; and England acquiesced, making such a translation a capital offense and burning at the stake anyone who owned even a partial copy of the Wycliffe Bible.

But under the dark surface of Rome's perceived order, the Spirit of God was moving. Soon, light—pages and pages of it—would burst onto the scene.

• • • • •

William Tyndale was born in the Cotswolds, one of my favorite areas in England. Located in the heart of the island, near the western edge of where England meets Wales, this south central region of the country is quintessentially English.

The word *Cotswolds* refers to sheep enclosures in rolling hillsides, and even today, the hills are dotted with flocks of sheep.

It's a homespun region, known for its hardworking people, good English wit, and pithy sayings. It's no surprise, then, that two of England's greatest literary men—Tyndale and Shakespeare—were born within sixty miles of each other and grew up in this hardy area of their country.

Tyndale appears to have been born into a family of some means. He eventually went to the University of Oxford, earning his Bachelor of Arts in 1512 and Master of Arts in 1515. Somewhere along the line, he was also ordained a priest.

It seems that after teaching for a year at Oxford, Tyndale went to Cambridge for further study. Interestingly, the great scholar Erasmus had been at Cambridge as a guest lecturer in both Greek and Theology from 1511–1514. Although Tyndale wasn't there at the same time as Erasmus, he would have had the opportunity at Cambridge to learn Greek from those who learned it from the best. Eventually, Tyndale would become one of the leading Greek scholars in the world, the others including such men as Erasmus, Martin Luther, and Philip Melanchthon—all who had a part in Bible translation.

The work of Erasmus is so intertwined with that of Tyndale's that a short sketch of Erasmus' life is helpful in understanding Tyndale's work.

Erasmus was born in Rotterdam, Holland, in 1466 as the illegitimate son of a priest. Both of his parents died when he was young, and he was raised in a monastery where he developed a love for learning. He later went to the University of Paris where he learned ancient Greek. His major life work which was most influential in the life of Tyndale was the gathering,

Cotswolds: The Cotswolds region of England, where William Tyndale grew up, is one of Terrie's and my favorites. William Shakespeare was also born near this area. Both men likely developed their ear for common English through their upbringing here.

comparing, and compiling Greek manuscripts for the New Testament into a single volume, referred to today as the *Textus Receptus,* or *Received Text.*

Prior to this time, the Roman Catholic Church, preferring the Latin Vulgate translation of the Bible (from which Wycliffe translated into English)—a fourth-century translation that was rife with translation errors—denied any scholars access to any ancient Greek manuscripts hidden in their vaults. Because of his intellect and scholastic ability, however, Erasmus was given access to the thousands of partial Greek manuscripts sealed in vaults across Europe. Recognizing the doctrinal bias of the Vulgate, he traveled throughout Europe (including Paris, England, France, the Netherlands, Italy, and Switzerland) gathering Greek texts, comparing them with one another, and compiling the verifiable manuscripts into a single volume.

Erasmus published the *Textus Receptus* from Holland in 1516, and with the help of the printing press, it quickly made its way to Greek-teaching universities across Europe, including, of course, Cambridge. This compiled manuscript was a major turning point in Bible translation across Europe. Luther translated from this text as would Tyndale and others.

Erasmus himself never fully repudiated the doctrine of the Catholic Church and took a confusing and inconsistent position in relation to the reformers. In theory, he sided with them; but in practice, he usually sided with the pope. He clearly stated his belief in salvation by grace and his conviction that the Bible should be translated into every vernacular language. (In fact, Tyndale's quote at the opening of this chapter was actually his paraphrase of a similar statement by Erasmus in the preface to the Greek New Testament.[1]) But when it came down to people actually *translating* and when the pope withstood them, Erasmus took a position that they should follow the wishes of the pope. For these and similar reasons, he is usually highly esteemed for his scholarship, but less favorably remembered otherwise.

Let's return to Tyndale in Cambridge. In 1517, as he read the Greek New Testament, Tyndale discovered what he had not heard in his years of study at Oxford, his upbringing in the Catholic Church, or his training for the priesthood. He read that salvation was a gift paid for completely by the precious blood of Christ, as of a lamb without blemish and without spot (1 Peter 1:19). He read that there was no way he could earn his salvation, but that it was a free gift of grace (Ephesians 2:8–9). As he read the New Testament, he found Christ. And from that moment on, Tyndale was a changed man.

• • • • •

Like many of us right after we trusted Christ as our Saviour, Tyndale was overcome with a desire to share the gospel. But as he talked with others, he quickly realized how ignorant they were of Scripture and how greatly they needed a Bible in their own language.

It's hard to believe, but common English was looked down upon in Tyndale's day by both the academic and religious worlds. Just as in Wycliffe's day, all university education was conducted in Latin, and the liturgy in church services was usually performed in Latin as well.

Of course the common, uneducated British man or woman did not know Latin. Thus, they quite literally were shut out from any spiritual content that might be included in an ordinary church service.

Tyndale believed that was wrong. He, who found Christ through the pages of the New Testament, believed every man, woman, and child should have access to that knowledge through the same source.

There was only one problem: translating the Bible into English was absolutely forbidden under penalty of death.

• • • • •

When you think of a zealous man, do you picture a firebrand with all flame and little substance? Do you envision a martyr-complex ready to exhaust itself in one supreme moment of glory?

Jesus was neither, yet John 2:17 (quoting from Psalm 69:9) says of Him, "The zeal of thine house hath eaten me up." Isaiah 59:17 prophesied of Christ, "For he put on righteousness as a breastplate, and an helmet of salvation upon his head; and he put on the garments of vengeance for clothing, *and was clad with zeal as a cloak.*"

Tyndale was a man with a deep passion for God's Word and a burning zeal to see it in the hands of every Englishman. But he was a thoughtful and measured man.

Tyndale was brilliant. He would eventually be fluent in seven languages—English, French, German, Italian, Greek, Latin, and Hebrew. But at Cambridge, he grew weary of endless discussion and theological debate with no action. On the other hand, if he were to take the action he sensed was needed, he would first need a place to quietly study God's Word and develop his own deep, settled convictions based on the Bible itself. To this end, he left Cambridge in 1521 and took a position as a tutor to two young boys in a home not far from where he grew up.

Little Sodbury, as the home of Sir John and Lady Walsh was known, often entertained guests of importance, and the Walshes always included Tyndale at the dinner table and in the discussions. Soon, his biblical views—not to mention his skill in articulating them or the fact that he always referred back to Scripture as his authority—became known.

King's College, Cambridge University: Tyndale earned both his Bachelor of Arts (1512) and Master of Arts (1515) at Oxford University. It is believed that he afterward went to one of the colleges at Cambridge University where he learned Greek from some of the leading Greek professors in England.

On Tyndale's days off, he would sometimes travel the fifteen miles to Bristol to preach. (Interestingly, this is the same city in which George Müller would pastor a church and open orphanages some 350 years later.) As Tyndale preached salvation by grace and expounded Scripture passages, a result was that he exposed the ungodly practices of the Catholic Church. For this, he was called to appear before John Bell, chancellor of the diocese of Worcester. Although no official charges were made, the point was clear—the Church was aware of his preaching and would not tolerate it. Tyndale's days at Little Sodbury were numbered.

The emphatic closure came when some clergy were having dinner at the Walshes' table, and, as was common, a theological debate with Tyndale ensued. Frustrated at Tyndale's ready Bible answers and the skillful way in which he pointed out the contradictions between Scripture and the Church, the clergyman finally spat out, "We had better be without God's laws than the Pope's!"

"I defy the Pope, and all his laws," Tyndale responded, "and if God spares my life, ere many years, I will cause the boy that driveth the plow to know more of the Scriptures than thou dost!"[2] Shortly after this incident, Tyndale left for London.

It was 1523, and it was time for action.

•   •   •   •   •

Tyndale could only entertain one shred of hope that he would be able to translate the Bible legally. And that was if the Bishop of London would specifically commission the translation. In theory, at least, this seemed possible. Bishop Tunstall loved Erasmus' work, and Erasmus himself had suggested the Bible should be translated into vernacular languages.

So Tyndale, prayerful and hopeful and armed with letters of recommendation from Sir John Walsh as well as his own translation of a Greek speech by Isocrates as an example of his ability, set off for London. This would be his first and only stay in England's capital city.

While waiting for an audience with the bishop, God brought Tyndale into contact with a man who would become a lifelong friend and supporter—Humphrey Monmouth, a Christian cloth merchant who loved God's Word and wanted to help Tyndale get it into English. For six months, Tyndale stayed in Monmouth's home. He was with all probability already translating the Bible during this time, while waiting for official permission.

When Tunstall finally called Tyndale, he listened to his proposal but turned him down. Tyndale was disappointed, but surely not surprised. And he was certainly not undecided.

Tyndale knew he could not stay in England and pursue the work to which God had called him, but he also knew that he must pursue this work. When Monmouth offered, most likely in early 1524, to send Tyndale across the English Channel to continue his work in Germany, he quickly and quietly left. It would be months before authorities in England even knew he was missing, and he would spend the remaining years of his life a hunted man in voluntary exile. He would never again set foot in his homeland.

* * * * *

In the spring of 1526, merchant ships docking in London began unloading the most precious cargo they had ever carried—three thousand completed copies of the New Testament in the English language. These little books, measuring roughly 6 3/4" by 4 1/4", arrived buried in sacks of flour and bales of cloth or sealed in watertight boxes in barrels of oil. From the docks, they were peddled by Lollard Christians across the nation.

And they were cheap. For one shilling and eightpence, anyone could buy an unbound copy, and for an extra shilling a bound copy. This economy was by design. Tyndale was a scholar, but he translated for the common laborer. His language was clear and crisp and easily understood. Thus it made sense also that his production would be economical for ease of access as well as small for ease of hiding. (After all, it was still illegal to own a copy of the Bible in English. In 1519, less than ten years before Tyndale translated the Bible, seven Christian parents were burned at the stake simply for teaching their children the Lord's Prayer in English.)[3]

This New Testament hadn't come without both exhaustion and peril for Tyndale. After leaving England, the next fifteen months were grueling. It seems he went briefly to Hamburg, then to Wittenberg, then back to Hamburg, then to Cologne—always working diligently at his translation while trying to stay one step ahead of anyone on his trail. Tyndale's longevity hinged on his ability to move quickly.

Finally, Tyndale had a completed manuscript, and in Cologne, he found a printer who was willing to take the risk to print it. But before the printer had finished the Gospel of Mark, the printing was discovered. By the providence of God, Tyndale and his assistant had just enough warning to grab armloads of unbound, printed sheets and slip out into the darkness.

From Cologne, they journeyed to Worms, and it was here where Tyndale's first full volumes would be printed and set sail for England.

England would never again be without a copy of God's Word.

• • • • •

Back in London, the New Testaments were gladly received. From the merchants to the universities to the countryside, people bought up copies of God's Word and for the first time in their lives read Scripture. Tyndale's vision for the plowboy was realized.

Not everyone in England was pleased, however. Cardinal Wolsey called a meeting of bishops in October to determine what could be done to stop the spread of the English New Testament. They determined that burning copies of it would be appropriate, with a threat to also burn those who possessed it.

God's Word isn't so easily stopped, however. In Isaiah 55:11, God promises, "So shall my word be that goeth forth out of my mouth: it shall not return unto me void, but it shall accomplish that which I please, and it shall prosper in the thing whereto I sent it."

Printing Press: The invention of the printing press greatly aided the spread of God's Word as translations began taking place throughout Europe. It would not be until 1540, however, that the Bible would be printed in England. Tyndale's work was printed on the continent and smuggled into England.

And the New Testament did prosper in England, fanning the flames of the reformation. Although some of the earliest gospel preachers of the English reformation had already staggered under Cardinal Wolsey's pressure and briefly recanted, the arrival of the New Testament in English put fresh iron in their blood. Soon, men and women who loved Christ more than their very lives would go to the stake quoting God's Word in English to strengthen themselves and share the gospel with onlookers.

As Tyndale continued to translate, he made time also to write encouragement to friends as well as tracts and books on Christian growth. Additionally, he wrote to answer both the charges of heresy the Church made against him and the public condemnations of his translation. (To discourage people from reading the New Testament, Bishop Tunstall wrote that Tyndale's translation had over two thousand errors. Tyndale wrote in his book *The Obedience of a Christian Man* that they were so concerned about making him a heretic that if he failed to dot an *i* in one of his printed translations, they would denounce it as heresy. In fact, however, part of the "error count" was due to Tunstall having the Latin Vulgate and Tyndale having the Greek. Tyndale's translation corrected what the Vulgate had gotten wrong.)

More important than answering his critics, however, Tyndale still had much work before him in translating the Bible. In the preface to his first translation, he had acknowledged that his work had been fast, and he promised a revision. Second, he had the entire Old Testament before him. Somehow, over the same fifteen months in which he was translating the New Testament, he took it upon himself to learn Hebrew, most likely from a rabbi in one of the German cities through which he traveled. And all the while, he maintained pastoral ministry to the poor and to other English religious refugees on the continent. He worked tirelessly five days a week and engaged the other two in ministry as his "pastime."

Still on the run, Tyndale moved from Worms to Antwerp. With the first five books of the Old Testament translated, he once again sought to avoid capture by taking a ship to Hamburg where he intended to have Genesis through Deuteronomy printed. The ship wrecked en route, and Tyndale lost everything—his translation of the Pentateuch included.

In Hamburg, however, Tyndale connected with Miles Coverdale, a friend who would prove to be of unforeseen assistance in the future.

Indefatigable, Tyndale began again with Genesis 1:1. By the end of 1529, the Pentateuch was ready for press, and by summer 1530, it reached England. Tyndale returned to Antwerp and continued translating. In 1534, he finished his revision of the New Testament.

• • • • •

In 1535, still in Antwerp, Tyndale met Henry Phillips, a man who, unknown to Tyndale, was sent specifically to find and capture him. Phillips won Tyndale's trust and some weeks later suggested they go out for lunch. En route, after asking to borrow the money Tyndale carried with him, Phillips betrayed him to agents lying in wait. He was taken to the Castle of Vilvorde in Belgium where he was imprisoned.

Tyndale spent the next year in the castle's dungeon. John Foxe reports of the imprisonment, "So powerful was Tyndale's doctrine and the godliness of his life, that during the year and a half of his imprisonment, it is said that he converted the jailer and his daughter and several others of his household."[4] During this time in prison, he also wrote his final book, *Faith Alone Justifies before God.*

On October 6, 1536, Tyndale was taken to the stake where he was strangled before being burnt. Just before he was executed, he cried out, "Lord, open the King of England's eyes!"[5]

• • • • •

Less than one year after Tyndale died, King Henry VIII licensed the first official English Bible. This Bible, known today as the Matthew's Bible, was comprised of Tyndale's translation of the New Testament as well as all he had completed of the Old Testament (from Genesis to part of Chronicles as well as many of the Psalms and the book of Jonah), with the remainder of the Old Testament having been translated by Myles Coverdale.

Nearly a century later, a new team of translators would undertake translating the Bible from Hebrew and Greek into English. Among their study sources was Tyndale's translation.

His translation, in fact, was so strong and precise that 90 percent of the New Testament and 75 percent of his work on the Old Testament is found verbatim in our King James Version.[6] And although the King James Version gives no acknowledgment to its primary translator—the only one of its translators who worked while living in exile, on the run, always poor, and often hungry—we can be sure that Tyndale would not mind. For Tyndale did not labor for himself. Throughout his short life, when accused by Catholic or English authorities that his translation was inaccurate or that he, in translating, was disloyal to his king, he readily responded that he would be more than happy to cease immediately, if only someone else would undertake the work. Fulfilling God's calling on his life was not a pursuit of self-expression; it was rooted in a love for God's Word, a conviction for the gospel, and above all, a love for Christ Himself.

Although Tyndale didn't live to see the English Bible welcomed into England's public arena, his life had made it possible.

TRUTHS FOR OUTSIDERS

What do we learn from the life of William Tyndale?

Count the cost of serving Christ. When Tyndale made his decision to translate the Bible into English, he was still at Little Sodbury. He did what he could to have the opportunity to translate with the sanction of the government, but when that was not granted, he was under no optimistic delusion of what it would cost him to move forward in this work. Although he could not have known the specifics of the hardships that would come, he knew they would be there. He counted the cost and decided that full surrender to the Lord's will was worth it.

One can imagine that as he left England, never to return to his homeland, he could have had Acts 20:22–24 in his mind: "And now, behold, I go bound in the spirit unto Jerusalem, not knowing the things that shall befall me there: Save that the Holy Ghost witnesseth in every city, saying that bonds and afflictions abide me. But none of these things move me, neither count I my life dear unto myself, so that I might finish my course with joy, and the ministry, which I have received of the Lord Jesus, to testify the gospel of the grace of God."

Don't waste time. Perhaps the most underrated accomplishment of Tyndale's life is the speed at which he learned and worked. While living almost as a fugitive exile, always on the move, he diligently made progress at his New Testament translation and still found time to learn Hebrew.

Tyndale would have had every reason to procrastinate, and he would have had legitimate reasons to slow down. Translating and studying languages in dark rooms with poor lighting, often cold and hungry, couldn't have been pleasant. But Tyndale had a passion for getting God's Word into English that ran deeper than a momentary rush of adrenaline. He worked efficiently, tirelessly, and persistently.

Never underestimate the power of Scripture. I know we keep coming back to a truth related to the power of God's Word. But it is no accident that every great moving of God leading out of the Dark Ages of Europe was preceded by God's Word in a common language. Hebrews 4:12 tells us, "For the word of God is quick, and powerful, and sharper than any twoedged sword, piercing even to the dividing asunder of soul and spirit, and of the joints and marrow, and is a discerner of the thoughts and intents of the heart."

Although Tyndale ministered to others, he never pastored a congregation. Although he discipled and taught others, he never taught in a seminary. Although he shared the gospel, he baptized no converts. But Tyndale loved and propagated God's Word, and he changed a nation for God.

HUGH LATIMER &
NICHOLAS RIDLEY

(Martyred October 16, 1555)

"Be of good comfort, Master Ridley, and play the man; we
shall this day light such a candle, by God's grace, in England,
as I trust shall never be put out."

Hugh Latimer

Broad Street in Oxford, England, locally known as "The Broad,"
does brisk business during the college months. Along the
south side stand rows of shops—Waterstones, Boswells, Fudge
Kitchen, Bravissimo, The Buttery, The Varsity Shop, Flaggs—
and on the other side are buildings for Balliol College, Oxford. The south
side is lined with outdoor tables and seating for some of the eateries, while
the north side—the college side—is often lined with parked bicycles, with
a few parallel parked cars interspersed.

In the center of the street, in the midst of pedestrian, bicycle, and auto
traffic, there is a cutout into asphalt revealing a cobbled patch of road
underneath. In the cobblestone is a black granite cross, which marks the

place of the stake at which were burned "the Oxford Martyrs"—Hugh Latimer and Nicolas Ridley in 1555, and then Thomas Cranmer in 1556.

In the wall of one of the college buildings, is a stone engraved with the following inscription:

> Opposite this point
> near the Cross in the
> middle of Broad Street
> HUGH LATIMER
> *one time Bishop of Worcester,*
> NICHOLAS RIDLEY
> *Bishop of London,* and
> THOMAS CRANMER
> *Archbishop of Canterbury,*
> were burnt for their faith in 1555 and 1556.

If you walk west along the street and then turn north at Magdalen Street, you'll see before you a large, spired monument, The Martyrs Memorial, erected in the memory of these men.

The names *Latimer and Ridley* roll off our tongues as if they were the first and last names of one man, with a conjunction serving as an odd middle name. They were, however, two men who were different in many respects, including a nearly two-decade difference in age.

What originally bound these men together was commitment to the cause of Christ, and what finally bound them together was a shared stake at which they were simultaneously martyred.

•   •   •   •   •

Hugh Latimer was born sometime between 1480–1494. (John Foxe suggests 1485; a more recent biographer suggests 1492.) In any case, the most important year of his life is 1524.

Cobblestone in Broad Street: The stones in the center of the street mark the spot where Latimer and Ridley were burned at the stake.

Latimer had just received his Bachelor of Divinity degree at Cambridge University. He was already a fellow at Clare College, Cambridge. He had received his Master of Arts in 1514 and was ordained a priest in 1515. In 1522 he had been nominated to the positions of university preacher and university chaplain.

At this point, Latimer was Catholic through and through. He described himself as "obstinate a papist as any was in England, insomuch that when I should be made bachelor of divinity, my whole oration was against Philip Melanchthon."

Philip Melanchthon was Martin Luther's assistant and collaborator and is remembered as the first systematic theologian of the Protestant Reformation. Luther had nailed his *Ninety-Five Theses* to the door in Wittenburg just seven years before Latimer's disputation for his divinity degree. The Reformation was quickly picking up steam on the European continent, and, as you can imagine, it had gained the attention of theologians in England as well.

Latimer, in particular, would have been interested, in part, because of his commitment to Catholicism. But my hunch is that he also chose this subject because of his penchant for controversy. Latimer was a tremendous public speaker, and he often used the controversial edge of a topic to stir interest in his listeners.

But gifted and respected as Latimer was, he was lost. The Lord used a quiet man, Thomas Bilney, to show Latimer the way of salvation. Bilney is sometimes called "The Spiritual Father of the Reformation in England" because of his influence on so many of the others who became spokesmen for the Reformation, especially Latimer.

Bilney sought private audience with Latimer and asked if he might confess to him as a priest. In his "confession," he poured out the gospel— that he knew himself to be a sinner, had tried all the prescribed means of grace set forth by the Catholic Church but without peace, how he had begun reading the New Testament and came to 1 Timothy 1:15: "This is a faithful saying, and worthy of all acceptation, that Christ Jesus came into the world to save sinners; of whom I am chief." When he read these words, the blinders fell off his eyes and the light appeared as he realized that *Jesus died to pay for his sins.* All there was for him to do was to cry out to Jesus alone for salvation.

As Bilney shared his testimony, the Holy Spirit worked in Latimer's heart. He saw his own sin and the futility of his own works. And he, too, saw the way of salvation through Christ. That day, God used an unassuming soulwinner to light the candle of the gospel in Latimer's spiritual darkness.

Latimer began preaching the blood of Christ alone as the sufficient atonement for sin. For the time being, he still believed in the authority of the pope and the Church, and for those reasons he saw concepts such as purgatory and the sacraments as valid. But he did not believe they atoned for sin. In later years, he recognized that none of these were biblical concepts, and he courageously defended this position before his execution.

Latimer is remembered primarily for his preaching. He is often referred to as "Apostle to the English" and "Preacher of the English Reformation." He was a gifted preacher as well as a godly man. His testimony, ability to explain Scripture, and gift for captivating an audience all helped to give him an ear in pulpits across England. From St. George's Chapel at Windsor Castle to St. Edward's Church at Cambridge University to country churches across his parish, Latimer preached salvation by Christ alone. And, except when preaching at Cambridge, he preached in English rather than Latin, another fact that endeared him to his audiences.

Remember that Latimer lived during years of incredible upheaval in England. The tumultuous marriages of King Henry VIII created significant political intrigue through which Latimer, a gospel preacher, actually became the court chaplain and eventually the Bishop of Worcester. To be sure, there was great opposition to Latimer's preaching. But the political climate of Henry VIII actually wanting to separate from the Catholic Church (to be able to divorce his wife) combined with Latimer's shrewd ability to perceive loopholes and make friends in high places allowed Latimer to preach in relative freedom—at least until the King no longer had need of him.

Eventually, Henry VIII determined to move his newly formed church more closely to Catholic doctrine and in 1539 insisted that all bishops sign his "Six Articles." Signing the articles meant affirming a belief in transubstantiation (that the bread and wine of communion became the literal body and blood of Christ and that then receiving that communion is how Christ is literally "received" for salvation), in the celibacy of priests, and in mass and confession to a priest as necessary for salvation.

Tower of London: Latimer and Ridley were both imprisoned in the Tower from September 1553–March 1554 as they awaited their heresy trials.

By this time, Latimer did not agree with any of these beliefs and protested them. As a result, he was forced to resign as bishop. Eventually, he was accused of heresy and imprisoned in the Tower of London. This seems to have been in the months preceeding Henry VIII's death, as Latimer was released once Edward VI was crowned.

During Edward VI's reign, England moved back toward Protestantism, and Latimer was again one of the court preachers. (The last sermon he preached for Edward VI was 3–4 hours long, and he held his audience for the duration.) During this relatively quiet period of Latimer's life, he refused to be made bishop again because he wanted to be free to preach his conscience. He preached wherever he was invited and enjoyed several years of fruitful ministry.

All of this would end when Edward VI died and Queen Mary I, today referred to as Bloody Mary, took the throne.

•   •   •   •   •

Nicholas Ridley's birth year is no more certain than Latimer's, but many historians place it around 1502. Ridley followed a similar academic trail as Latimer at Cambridge University, only through Pembroke College, rather than Clare. Also, Ridley had an added advantage of education in Paris. This took place after he earned his Master of Arts and became a priest. He probably encountered Reformation discussion and ideas while he was in France.

After returning to Cambridge, Ridley went on to earn his Bachelor of Divinity in 1537 (thirteen years after Latimer). He would later earn a Doctor of Divinity in 1541.

In 1540, Ridley became one of the king's chaplains, and in 1547 he was made the Bishop of Rochester. At this point, Latimer was already the Bishop of Worcester, and Thomas Cranmer was the Archbishop of Canterbury. As advocators of reform, the three were well acquainted and worked together on various projects. (Cranmer would later be imprisoned with Latimer and Ridley in the Tower of London and was martyred in the same place as they, five months later.)

If Latimer is remembered as a preacher, Ridley is remembered as a scholar. To be sure, both preached and both were incredibly learned men. But Ridley's gifts lay in study and in his ability to assimilate concepts from a variety of sources and from them articulate his own clear ideas.

Ridley memorized all of the New Testament epistles in Greek. His preaching was full of Scripture. And his debate skills were sharp and full of wit.

During the questioning of Latimer, Ridley, and Cranmer under Queen Mary, one of their interrogators complained in exasperation, "Latimer leaneth to Cranmer, Cranmer to Ridley, and Ridley to the singularity of his own wit: so that if you overthrow the singularity of Ridley's wit, then must needs the religion of Cranmer and Latimer fall also."[1]

This wasn't true—the three all leaned to Scripture—but Ridley had helped the three articulate their scriptural arguments in an unusual time and fashion.

When Latimer and Ridley were imprisoned in London Tower, at first, they were carefully kept separate. Latimer had a servant, Augustine

Bernher, who was allowed to attend not only to Latimer, but to others as well. A faithful and courageous man, Bernher relayed messages back and forth between Latimer and Ridley.

To prepare for the trial which he knew was coming, Ridley determined to write out his arguments against the Catholic concept of transubstantiation. This short treatise became a tract titled *A Brief Declaration of the Lord's Supper,* and due to the work of Bernher, it was published in Germany shortly after Latimer's death.

Meanwhile, Ridley also took upon himself to write an eleven-point rebuttal of the mass. Through Bernher, he sent this to Latimer for his comments. Latimer made notes in the margin and added an essay of his own as an appendix, which were then sent back to Ridley. Ridley adjusted, sent back to Latimer, and so forth. (This too was published in Germany shortly after the death of Latimer and Ridley, thanks to Bernher.)

In this manner, Ridley developed a systematic rebuttal of the claims that would be placed against him, Latimer refined the arguments, and both were strengthened.

Not long after this exchange, due to the influx of Protestant prisoners under Queen Mary, Cranmer, Latimer, and Ridley were all placed in the same cell. The men were cold and hungry and could not have enjoyed the putrid odors of an overcrowded prison without ventilation. But they appreciated each other's company and fellowship. And they, no doubt, discussed the scriptural points needed to answer the charges which would soon be officially made against them.

But we're getting ahead of the story.

• • • • •

When Mary I ascended to the throne, persecution came swiftly. Even before her coronation, she had already sent several men, including

Latimer, Ridley, and Cranmer, to the Tower. (Cranmer was especially marked by Mary because of the political role he had played in securing Henry VIII's divorce from his first wife, who was also Mary's mother, as well as Cranmer's support for Lady Jane Grey's nine-day reign between Edward VI and Mary.) During Mary's five-year reign, she would have 288 religious dissenters burned at the stake.

The three were imprisoned in the Tower from September 1553 to March 1554, when they were taken to Oxford and waited in Bocardo, a notorious Oxford prison, before they would be called to stand trial.

The trial was specifically designed to ridicule the defendants and their views, particularly their views against transubstantiation. The entire ordeal had been carefully arranged to appear as if it were a formal debate between the leading scholars of Catholic traditions, specifically transubstantiation and mass, who would be hearing the weak arguments of the opposing side. In reality, it was a trial for heresy.

The men were called in individually before the council to state their position. Cranmer first, then Ridley both set forth their views and were ordered to debate on the Monday and Tuesday of the following week respectively. Latimer said simply that he was an old man and could not sustain a substantive debate, but that he had read through the New Testament seven times since his imprisonment and could find no mention of the mass or of communion becoming Christ's body. He was silenced and ordered to appear for debate the following Wednesday.

The debates went as might be expected. They were conducted in Latin. All three men complained that the debates were non-substantive with their opponents regularly losing their tempers, shouting down the remarks of the defendants, and going off into tangents. In the end, all three were condemned as heretics and sentenced to be burned at the stake.

Ridley pointed out that this sentence would send him sooner to Heaven than would have happened otherwise. Latimer, who really was up in years for that time in history, responded, "I thank God most heartily, that He hath prolonged my life to this end, that I may in this case glorify God by that kind of death."[2]

The men were taken to separate prisons where they were held for another eighteen months under constant tension that every day could be the day they would burn. While they waited, others were martyred in increasing numbers.

Finally, Latimer and Ridley were called for a last examination, giving them one last opportunity to recant. (Cranmer's case was delayed due to formalities of him being an archbishop. His last examination and sentencing came two months after their deaths, and he was executed five months after them.)[3]

The night before the men were to be burned at the stake, Ridley's brother visited him and offered to spend the night with him. Ridley declined, saying, "I intend to go to bed, and to sleep as quietly tonight as ever I did."[4]

The following day, October 16, 1555, Latimer and Ridley were taken from their respective prison houses and met as they were led to the stake, just outside of the old city walls.

A Catholic bishop preached against their heresy—the men were not allowed to answer him—and they mounted the platform to be chained. Ridley's brother-in-law had brought two small bags of gunpowder which he was allowed to tie around the neck of each man to hasten their death.

As the fire was lit, Latimer said his famous last words to Ridley: "Be of good comfort, Master Ridley, and play the man; we shall this day light such a candle, by God's grace, in England, as I trust shall never be put out."[5]

Latimer died quickly. Ridley suffered in agony as the fire burned his lower body but refused to burn higher. Finally, both men were in the presence of Christ.

The gospel candle they gave their lives to light, however, continued to burn. Over the following years, it grew and spread across England.

TRUTHS FOR OUTSIDERS

What do we learn from the lives of Hugh Latimer and Nicholas Ridley? **Be faithful as a soulwinner.** The soulwinning efforts of Thomas Bilney remind us that not all that is done for God is done behind a pulpit. Bilney led the man who would become "the Apostle to the English" to Christ. J. C. Ryle wrote, "No one of the Reformers probably sowed the seeds of Protestant doctrine so widely and effectually among the middle and lower classes as Latimer."[6] But it was Thomas Bilney who led Latimer to Christ. You never know when you share the gospel with someone how the Lord may use them in the future.

When you teach or preach, make truth accessible to others. For Latimer and Ridley, this meant preaching in English rather than in Latin to people who did not speak Latin. For me as a pastor, it means diligent study and carefully thought-through application for the specific audience to whom I'm preaching. For example, when I preach in our Christian school's elementary chapel, I need to work to apply the truth differently than when I am preaching in a Sunday morning service or when I am leading a Bible study at our nearby military base.

Whether you teach Sunday school, one-on-one discipleship, or your own children, it's not enough to simply throw the truth out there. We must do our best to make it accessible and applicable to those we teach.

Love for God's Word is cultivated in personal study. Both Latimer and Ridley practiced the discipline of personal devotional time in Scripture. They rose long before daybreak to spend the early hours of the day in deep study of the Scriptures and in prayer. In this, they followed the example of Christ: "And in the morning, rising up a great while before day, he went out, and departed into a solitary place, and there prayed" (Mark 1:35).

God gives grace in the face of martyrdom. I suppose because we in the United States have faced little that could be called real persecution, we don't fully grasp the vastness of God's grace in the face of death. But as I study the lives of men like Latimer and Ridley, not to mention women like Anne Askew who were tortured and martyred about the same time they were, my confidence in God's ability to sustain me in these kinds of situations grows. Jesus, who "became obedient unto death, even the death of the cross" (Philippians 2:8), gave this message of comfort and hope to the persecuted church at Smyrna: "Fear none of those things which thou shalt suffer: behold, the devil shall cast some of you into prison, that ye may be tried; and ye shall have tribulation ten days: be thou faithful unto death, and I will give thee a crown of life" (Revelation 2:10).

7

PATRICK HAMILTON
(1504–1528)

"The reek of master Patrick Hamilton affected all those
upon whom it blew."

John Lindsay, *servant to Archbishop Beaton*
after the burning of Patrick Hamilton

S t. Andrews, Scotland, is a town rich with history. It is the home of the University of St. Andrews, the third oldest institution in the English-speaking world. (You may remember from recent history that Prince William and Kate Middleton first met while both students at this university.)

Additionally, Scotland is the birthplace of golf. And the town of St. Andrews, in particular, is the paradise of golf. Its rolling hills and stunning views make it a perfect place for the six annual golf tournaments it hosts. When Terrie and I were in Scotland a few summers ago, it seemed the town was consumed with golf. Everywhere we went, there were golfers and golf tourists and golf memorabilia and golf advertisements and golf everything.

We had a few free hours one afternoon and decided to take a walk down by the University of St. Andrews. Weaving through the crowds of tourists, we found ourselves near the university entrance looking down on a granite monogram of the initials *PH* in the cobblestone pavement. This was our introduction to Patrick Hamilton—the extraordinary young man who was burned in that very spot almost five centuries earlier. We would soon discover that Patrick Hamilton, hardly older than the median-age student currently at St. Andrews, was as consumed with the gospel as the entire town was currently ablaze with golf. The flames that eventually consumed his body were allowed because of his deliberate, willing sacrifice for Christ.

• • • • •

Patrick Hamilton was born into Scottish nobility. The second son of Sir Patrick Hamilton and Catherine Stewart, he was the great-grandson of King James II. This made him a distant cousin to Scottish King James V, who was the fifteen-year-old regent at the time of Hamilton's martyrdom.

At the age of fourteen, Hamilton left for study abroad at the University of Paris. There, he earned his Master of Arts in 1520, when he was just seventeen years old.

Even more significantly, however, it was at the University of Paris where Hamilton heard the gospel. Luther had nailed his *Ninety-Five Theses* to the church door in Wittenburg just two years earlier, and neither Luther's books nor conversations about them were hard to come by. Hamilton studied, asked questions, and came to see for himself the simple reality of salvation by grace alone.

When the University of Paris publicly burned Martin Luther's books in an attempt to stem the tide of the ideas they spread, Hamilton went to the University of Leuven in what is now Belgium to study under Erasmus, who had just published the Greek New Testament five years prior.

Whether Hamilton made his decision to trust Christ as his personal Saviour in Paris or Leuven, we aren't sure, but we know that when he returned to Scotland in 1523, he was a saved man. And he was a man with a message.

· · · · ·

Hamilton was just nineteen years old when he joined the faculty of arts at the University of St. Andrews. He seems to have had musical talents and conducted his own compositions in the cathedral. To the average observer, Hamilton was a highly-motivated, accomplished young man destined, no doubt, for greatness.

To the students who had private spiritual conversation with Hamilton, however, his future seemed less certain. For Hamilton was intent, not just to personally believe the gospel, but to lead others to Christ. This was, of course, a dangerous course of action.

Strictly speaking, Hamilton wasn't alone in his witness, for Martin Luther's books were also finding their way into Scotland. And the arrival of Tyndale's New Testaments in 1526 was a game changer. The English New Testament, though still promptly banned, was privately circulated and discussed, giving Hamilton increased ability to share the gospel as he could use Scripture itself in English.

Hamilton's gospel efforts did not go unnoticed, and by early 1527, they came to the attention of James Beaton, Archbishop of St. Andrews. In April of that year, Beaton summoned Hamilton to stand trial under the accusation of heresy.

· · · · ·

Hamilton had little doubt how a heresy trial would end. He had taught against salvation by works, transubstantiation, prayers to saints, and other

Catholic doctrine. Most importantly, he had taught that salvation is a gift of God's grace received by faith alone. But before publicly defending these truths in a debate trial with doctors of theology, he wanted to work out a sound scriptural framework. Thus, he fled to Germany to have time to solidify his convictions.

In Germany, Hamilton enrolled in the brand new University of Marburg, which opened May 30, 1527. Over the next six months, he studied God's Word and wrote his only book, *Patrick's Places*, a doctrinal thesis of his faith. The book differentiates between the law and grace and correctly points out that God's law is necessary to reveal our sin (Romans 7:7), but it falls short of bringing us salvation. He points out that good works cannot save a person and our sinful works reveal that we have sinful hearts

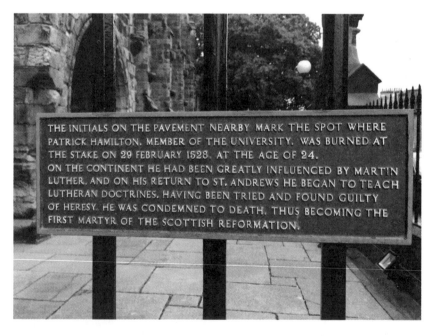

Plaque at St. Andrew: Patrick Hamilton was martyred at the age of twenty four. His monogram in the pavement outside the University of St. Andrews (opposite page) as well as the nearby plaque are passed daily by students roughly the same age.

(Matthew 12:33). He goes on to describe the necessity of justification by grace alone and points out specifically how the Catholic Church—in both doctrine and practice—undermines and directly opposes these truths. Needless to mention, the book did not earn him favor with the powerful Archbishop Beaton.

In late fall of 1527, Hamilton returned to Scotland with his mind convinced, his heart settled, and his faith firm. Many encouraged him to remain in Germany, but although he knew he may be killed for preaching the gospel, he was burdened for the Scots to hear the gospel. He returned then with one purpose—to preach the gospel to as many people as he could in his lifetime.

• • • • •

Rather than returning to the University of St. Andrews on the eastern side of Scotland, Hamilton traveled to the western side of the island. There, at his brother's house in Kincavel, he shared the gospel with his family and saw his mother, brother, sister, and other relatives come to faith in Christ. From there, he went to Linlithgow, about twenty miles west of Edinburgh, married, and continued his work as an itinerant soulwinner.

Back at St. Andrews, Archbishop Beaton was eager to quietly bring Hamilton back in such a way as to not sound off an alarm to the general public or Hamilton's connections in the King's court. He developed an elaborate scheme, inviting Hamilton to return to the University and guaranteeing full freedom to teach anything Patrick would like as well as to preach openly. He hoped that this would make the entire town witnesses of Hamilton's heresy.

Hamilton saw through the ruse and predicted to his close friends that he would soon die a martyr's death. But he accepted the invitation as an opportunity to openly share the gospel. He also wanted the entire town to hear his preaching, although for vastly conflicting reasons than the Archbishop's.

• • • • •

Hamilton arrived in St. Andrews mid-January of 1528. In addition to his teaching duties, he was instructed to meet with Friar Alexander Alesius to explain his doctrinal concerns so the Church would have opportunity to correct herself where wrong. Once again, Hamilton was not fooled, but rather than viewing Alesius as his enemy, he saw him as a lost man in need of Christ. God used Hamilton's witness in Alesius' life to raise doubt in his previous beliefs. He eventually trusted Christ and after Hamilton's death became his first biographer.

Without the anticipated help from Alesius, Beaton sent another friar, Alexandar Campbell, to interview Hamilton. Campbell listened closely, sympathetically agreed with all of Hamilton's grievances with Catholic doctrine . . . and took his findings directly to Beaton to be used in Hamilton's eventual trial.

Hamilton was allowed to preach and teach for about five weeks. But in the predawn hours of February 29, 1528, he heard a knock on his door. He was arrested and called to an immediate trial at St. Andrews Cathedral.

St. Andrews Castle: George Wishart was imprisoned in the Sea Tower of this castle, and he was burned just outside of its walls. A few months later, the first Protestant church in Scotland met inside the castle walls.

• • • • •

Determined to silence Hamilton by execution, Beaton knew he had to act quickly. Rather than Hamilton's preaching turning the town against his "heresy," as Beaton had hoped, it had drawn hearers to respond to the gospel. Additionally, if Beaton allowed a protracted trial or lengthy time between trial and execution, there was a strong possibility someone may intercede to the king (Hamilton's relative) on Hamilton's behalf.

Thus, in an unusual move, Beaton had Hamilton arrested, tried, condemned, and taken to his execution all in a matter of hours.

At Hamilton's trial, Friar Campbell, who had privately interviewed Hamilton, read the charges against him. Rather than denying the charges, Hamilton skillfully answered each with Scripture and sound logic. He emphasized that his teaching was from the Bible and pointed out that because God's Word had been withheld from the common people, they were unable to know the truths which the Church had corrupted.

As expected, Hamilton was convicted of heresy and sentenced to death by burning.

Because of the unusual speed in which he was arrested, tried, and convicted, the townspeople did not know, even as they followed Hamilton to the place of his execution, that he was to be burned. The crowd swelled en route, believing they were about to hear him preach.

* * * * *

Death by burning was a gruesome invention of the Dark Ages. The presupposition was that burning a heretic here on Earth spared him from eternal hellfire, allowing him to instead suffer in purgatory.

I've wondered sometimes how much pain martyrs felt as they were burned at the stake. Perhaps God, in His grace, eased their suffering. Indeed, often they had gunpowder tied around their necks so they would die as the first flames leapt up.

In Hamilton's case, however, there is no doubt that he felt the full impact of the flames.

Before Hamilton was tied to the stake, he gave his coat, gown, and hat to his servant saying, "These will not profit in the fire, they will profit thee. After this, of me thou canst receive no commodity, except the example of my death, which, I pray thee, bear in mind."[1]

The executioner tied gun powder around him and lit the fire. But a strong wind blew that day, and those who had built the fire used green wood. Those factors combined brought Hamilton excruciating suffering as he was six long hours in the flames before he died. Those who watched said he roasted rather than burned. Knox said that his last words were, "Lord Jesus, receive my spirit! How long shall darkness overwhelm this realm? How long wilt Thou suffer this tyranny of men?"[2]

• • • • •

The aftereffect of Hamilton's martyrdom was anything but what Archbishop Beaton had hoped for. As the shocked town of St. Andrews searched for an answer as to why Hamilton, whose preaching they had understood and enjoyed and whose testimony they had found unblemished, was thus executed, many trusted Christ as their Saviour.

After all, how do you watch a twenty-four-year-old young man with noble blood, accomplished talent and learning, and a bright future—a man who was convinced of his position in the truth, articulate in his defense of his faith, and patient in brutal martyrdom—and not at least consider if his preaching was valid?

The conversions resulting from Hamilton's martyrdom were so overwhelming in number that John Lindsay, servant to Archbishop Beaton, advised Beaton against future burnings saying, "The reek of master Patrick Hamilton affected all those upon whom it blew." The six hours of smoking torture had not been in vain.

• • • • •

As Hamilton carried out his few years of faithful preaching and witness and as he endured a torturous burning at the stake, he could not have known the fruit that God would bring through his consecration.

The second century Christian author Tertullian wrote, "The blood of the martyrs is the seed of the church."[3] Indeed, it seemed that way in Scotland.

Knox Statue and House: John Knox's house has been converted into a museum telling the remarkable story of the spread of the gospel in Scotland.

Eighteen years to the day (March 1, 1546) after Hamilton was burned at the stake, Scotland martyred another faithful Christian, George Wishart. For four years, Wishart had been preaching the gospel throughout Scotland, systematically moving from the east to the west. Finally, he was apprehended, presented for a show trial, condemned, and executed.

As is so often the case in service for God, although Hamilton and Wishart are not often remembered or known, Wishart's disciple, John Knox, is.

Knox, like many of the other reformers, was a Catholic priest who discovered the gospel through the study of Scripture. Through the influence of Wishart, Knox began preaching salvation by grace alone, the Bible as sole authority, and against Catholic mass and purgatory. Shortly after Wishart's death, Knox became pastor of a church in Scotland and was eventually imprisoned to French galley ships. Eventually he was released, went to England, and later back to Scotland. It was there that he led the Protestant Reformation in Scotland.

John Knox deeply depended on prayer. It was of supreme importance to him, as we see illuminated in two famous quotes, one about Knox, and the other by him. Mary, Queen of Scots, said of Knox, "I fear the prayers of John Knox more than all the assembled armies of Europe." And Knox himself famously prayed, "Give me Scotland, or I die."

Throughout the seventeenth and eighteenth centuries, and even into the early twentieth century, Scotland became known as a land of revival and missions. Mary Slessor (missionary to Africa), David Livingstone (missionary and explorer to Africa), and Eric Liddell (missionary to China) were just a few of the many notable Christians who would come from Scotland. The blood of the Scottish martyrs truly was the seed of the church.

TRUTHS FOR OUTSIDERS

What do we learn from the life of Patrick Hamilton? **Even the shortest life invested in eternity is worthwhile.** Having first encountered Hamilton's testimony in the midst of a golf-crazed town made his focus on eternal values that much clearer to me. Here was a young man who had every opportunity to become a worldly success, yet he loved Christ more. He said with the Apostle Paul, "While we look not at the things which are seen, but at the things which are not seen: for the things which are seen are temporal; but the things which are not seen are eternal" (2 Corinthians 4:18).

Hamilton's short life helps us peel back the layers of materialism and short-sighted aspirations in our own lives. It prompts us to evaluate if we are stewarding our lives for self or for eternity.

Hamilton had similar opportunities as Moses did in the palace, but, like Moses, he had his sights set higher: "Choosing rather to suffer affliction with the people of God, than to enjoy the pleasures of sin for a season; Esteeming the reproach of Christ greater riches than the treasures in Egypt: for he had respect unto the recompence of the reward" (Hebrews 11:25–26).

Christians who believe the Bible and share the gospel are offensive to the world. Moses, one of the Old Testament heroes of the faith to us, was a reproach to Egypt (Hebrews 11:26). Paul, whom Christians around the world highly esteem, was thought of as "the filth of the world . . . the offscouring of all things" (1 Corinthians 4:13) to unbelievers. Hamilton was so despised that John Lindsay referred to the smoke of his martyrdom as "the reek of master Patrick Hamilton."

None of us want to be despised. We don't want people to think of us as *filth* and *offscouring*—the outcasts and refuse of society.

Hamilton did nothing unkind or immoral to earn hatred. He simply sacrificed to share the gospel, and in doing so exposed the evil of others. As a result, they hated and killed him.

This should encourage us to not place our value in the approval of the world. Jesus Himself was "despised and rejected of men" (Isaiah 53:3), and if we "live godly in Christ Jesus," we "shall suffer persecution" (2 Timothy 3:12).

No one should wait until they are older to serve the Lord. Hamilton was martyred at the same age I was when I began pastoring. Many well-meaning Christians asked me if I was too young to take the responsibility of the pastorate. I fully felt the gravity of my responsibility, but I knew it was God who was calling me to do it. Over three decades later, I'm thankful I followed God's leading.

In whatever capacity God gives you the opportunity to serve, do it. Don't wait until later or until it is more convenient. And, especially if you are young, seize the day and serve Christ in your youth. "Let no man despise thy youth; but be thou an example of the believers, in word, in conversation, in charity, in spirit, in faith, in purity" (1 Timothy 4:12).

Study the Bible and understand the basis for your convictions. Hamilton was wise to thoroughly study his beliefs before he would be called to defend them. If we wait until the hour of ridicule or question to know the biblical reasons for what we believe, we will miss opportunities to present truth, and we may find ourselves wavering in conviction.

You may not write a doctrinal thesis, but you should "Study to shew thyself approved unto God, a workman that needeth not to be ashamed, rightly dividing the word of truth" (2 Timothy 2:15).

Trust God to use your life. There is no way Hamilton could have known how significant his martyrdom would be to the spread of the gospel in Scotland. The harvest of souls he had longed for came after his death. While we want our lives to make a difference and seek for the most effective ways to sow the gospel, we need to trust God with the results. He is the Lord of the harvest, and He both calls and rewards the efforts of His laborers (Matthew 9:38).

8

JOHN BUNYAN
(1628–1688)

"If I was out of prison today, I would preach the gospel again tomorrow by the help of God."

John Bunyan

When most of us hear the name *John Bunyan*, we immediately think of his most famous book and what remains today a perennial best seller, *Pilgrim's Progress*—an allegorical story of a man named Christian and his journey to the Celestial City.

It is striking to me that in the whole of the book, from the time Christian begins his journey at the Slough of Despond until the moment he crosses the river into the Celestial City, he is never given an overview of the remaining path ahead. He has no Pisgah moment of looking beyond and knowing what or how many stages of the journey remain. Rather, Bunyan allowed his fictional character to tread forward in much the same way as his author—one step at a time, sustained moment by moment, trusting in God's will and His way.

John Bunyan: Contemporaries described John Bunyan as a tall, broad-shouldered man with reddish hair and a voice that carried well when projected in preaching.

Of course, when we read of the life of John Bunyan today, we do so with the advantage of hindsight. How easy it is for us to condense Bunyan's twelve-year imprisonment, for instance, into a passing mention. How difficult it must have been for him to live out each of those days, never knowing how much longer his sentence would last.

Even so, Bunyan lived his life in much the same way as the protagonist in his classic—as a pilgrim en route to a celestial city. Bunyan's start to his journey, however, was significantly longer and less conventional than Christian's.

• • • • •

John Bunyan was born in 1628 in Elstow, Bedfordshire, to a tinker—a craftsman who repaired metal tools and utensils. His parents were poor, but they somehow managed to send John to school long enough that he learned to read and write. This literacy would be an invaluable gift throughout his life.

Even as a boy, Bunyan loved a good story. He grew up around the homespun storytelling of English peasants and early on developed the ability to skillfully weave a story of vivid imagery with everyday words. Along with his family John attended the Anglican church, which was by then the state church of England. He was a rare combination of a boy sensitive enough to fear the angry God who often appeared in his nighttime dreams but daring enough to purposefully provoke Him during the day through foul language.

When he was just fifteen years old, young Bunyan experienced the bitter loss of his mother and sister who died within a week of one another. Adding to Bunyan's heartache, his father remarried within a month, probably as much for practical reasons as any. In any case, Bunyan didn't get along well with his stepmother and joined Cromwell's army when he turned sixteen that fall. This was during the English Civil War as Cromwell fought for greater parliamentary rule while the loyalists fought for a strong monarchy.

Just before Bunyan was released from his three-year stint of duty, God spared his life in a remarkable way. He had been assigned to stand as sentinel, but a fellow soldier asked to swap duty nights with him. That very night, the man who stood in Bunyan's place was killed by enemy fire. Bunyan was shaken and years later would see this as the extraordinary providence of God, sparing his life for a special purpose.

When Bunyan was about twenty, he married and took up his father's occupation as his own. Although Bunyan and his wife had four children together, including a blind daughter named Mary, there is no written record of their marriage or of his wife's name. Even in Bunyan's autobiography, although he spoke warmly of his wife, he did not mention her name.

What he did mention, however, was that they were very poor—"as poor as poor might be (not having so much household stuff as a dish or a spoon betwixt us both)"[1]—and that she owned two Christian books which her godly father had given her before he died. Bunyan read these with her. And although he did not sense conviction at the time, God was already working in his heart.

Partly due to the sense of responsibility that came with marriage and partly to please his wife, Bunyan began going to church and made sincere efforts to reform his ways. But he soon found that he could not consistently live righteously. No matter how hard he tried, he not only had to wrestle with the outward sins for which he was so well known (swearing still among them), but he had his own sinful nature with which to contend.

Bunyan describes the struggles of his spiritual journey in his autobiography *Grace Abounding to the Chief of Sinners*. As you read this transparent testimony, you can't help but marvel at God's patience in his life. It seems that from one paragraph to the next he vacillated from a desire to be saved but not understanding the gospel to feeling that he was beyond hope and thus may as well abandon all efforts at self-reform.

In God's mercy, one day as Bunyan was walking to Bedford on a tinkering job, he passed by some ladies and overheard their conversation. They were talking about having been born again. Bunyan wrote:

> In one of the streets of that town, I came where there were three or four poor women sitting at a door, in the sun, talking about the things of God; and being now willing to hear them discourse, I drew near to hear what they said . . . Their talk was about a new birth, the work of God on their hearts, also how they were convinced of their miserable state by nature; they talked how God had visited their souls with His love in the Lord Jesus, and with what words and promises they had been refreshed, comforted, and supported . . . . And, methought, they spake as if joy did make them speak; they spake with such pleasantness of scripture language, and with such appearance of grace in all they said, that they were to me, as if they had found a new world . . . [2]

They continued to speak of God's comfort and presence through severe trials, and Bunyan couldn't restrain himself any longer. He interrupted to ask how he could know more.

The ladies directed Bunyan to their pastor, John Gifford. Even then, Bunyan wasn't a fast convert. For several months he wrestled with doubt over his past sins and constantly analyzed himself: did he love God enough or keep God's commandments well enough to actually consider himself a Christian? But finally, about a year after his first talk with Pastor Gifford, the glorious truth of the gospel finally broke through to Bunyan. He records in *Grace Abounding:*

> One day as I was walking into the field . . . this sentence fell upon my soul, "Thy righteousness is in heaven:" and methought withal, I saw, with the eyes of my soul, Jesus Christ at God's right hand; there, I say, was my righteousness; so that wherever I was, or whatever I was doing, God could not say of me, "He wants [lacks] my righteousness," for that was just before him. I also saw, moreover, that it was not my good frame of heart that made my righteousness better, nor yet my bad frame that made my righteousness worse; for my righteousness was Jesus Christ Himself, The same yesterday, to-day, and for ever (Hebrews 13:8).

> Now did my chains fall off my legs indeed; I was loosed from afflictions and irons; my temptations also fled away; so that . . . went I also home rejoicing for the grace and love of God.[3]

After salvation, Bunyan presented himself for baptism in the nonconformist church which Gifford pastored, and he moved his family to Bedford that they might be present at every service. Pastor Gifford took Bunyan under his wing and instructed him in assurance of salvation and Bible study. Pastor Gifford had no idea that he was helping to ground in the faith a man whose pen would reach the world.

•   •   •   •   •

In 1655, two years after Bunyan joined St. John's Church in Bedford, he was asked to give an extemporaneous testimony. His natural ability to clearly articulate biblical truth in a way that reached the hearts of his hearers was immediately apparent. From that day on, Bunyan knew God had called him to preach. With Pastor Gifford's help and instruction, Bunyan began as a layman, preaching throughout the week in open fields.

Bunyan grew extremely popular. One biographer said, "When the country understood, that . . . the tinker had turned preacher, they came to hear the word by hundreds, and that from all parts."[4] If it were announced ahead in what open field he would be preaching, people would arrive at sunrise to hear him at noon. Later in his ministry, if it were announced the day before that he would be preaching at 7:00 AM, there would be a crowd of 1,200 waiting to hear him.

His preaching was effective, too. John Owen, a nonconformist theologian and Bunyan's contemporary, said, "I would willingly exchange my learning for the tinker's power of touching men's hearts." A London businessman reported, "Mr. Bunyan preached so New Testament-like he made me admire and weep for joy, and give him my affections."[5]

Bunyan wasn't oblivious to this ability God had given him, but he did guard against the temptation of pride. Charles Spurgeon told about a time when a friend congratulated Bunyan after his message: "'You preached well,' said a friend to John Bunyan one morning. 'You are too late,' said honest John, 'The devil told me that before I left the pulpit.'"[6]

In addition to his preaching ministry, Bunyan began writing. He published his first book, *Some Gospel Truths Opened*, in 1656. It was primarily a doctrinal rebuttal of Quaker teachings that questioned the divinity of Christ as well as their reliance on a mystical inner light for spiritual direction. Bunyan's solid theological grounding even in his early Christian life is evident in this book. He strongly believed the Bible was the inspired and final revelation of God and felt great concern when he saw its authority undermined through any means of continuing revelation. Over the next thirty-two years, Bunyan would write prolifically, publishing a total of sixty books.

Three years after Bunyan began preaching, his wife of ten years died, leaving him a single father of four young children under the age of ten. Almost two years later, in 1659, he remarried. His second wife, Elizabeth, would prove to be an amazing woman of grace and strength in the days ahead.

• • • • •

When Bunyan began his ministry, Oliver Cromwell was Lord Protector of England, and there was a great degree of religious liberty for the nonconformists. But in 1658, Cromwell died, and his son, Richard, was given the title. Richard, however, wasn't up to the task and formally relinquished his position nine months later. In 1660, Parliament invited the exiled Charles II to return to England and restore the monarchy.

As a result of King Charles II's return, the Church of England was once again the national church, and nonconformists groups were disallowed from meeting. These were challenging days for independent churches, and yet, they were days during which the gospel was spreading.

For instance, New Park Street Baptist Chapel (where Charles Spurgeon would later pastor) was founded in 1650. One year previously, the first Baptist church in Wales was established in the village of Ilston in 1649. The church was founded by and pastored for several years by John Myles. Not long after its beginning, the church relocated to the nearby town of Swansea, Wales. Myles continued as the pastor until he fled persecution by immigrating to the American Colonies. He, along with several members from the church in Wales, established a Baptist church in Swansea, Massachusetts, in 1663—the earliest Baptist church in the state. The church in Wales continued to meet in secret, eventually changing its name to Bethesda Baptist Chapel.

Back in Bedford, Bunyan's home church, St. John's, had to meet in secret. Bunyan himself continued his nearby preaching ministry, doing his best not to attract attention.

In November of 1660, Bunyan was scheduled to preach in a friend's home some thirteen miles from Bedford. A friend warned him that a warrant was out for his arrest and urged him to escape. Bunyan, as well as anyone else, could see that tough times for dissenters in England were ahead, and he didn't want gospel preachers to flee the country at the first sign of trouble. Furthermore, he knew he couldn't live in hiding; he *had* to preach. Wanting to encourage others to live boldly, he preached that morning. He was arrested midway through his message. And so began what would turn out to be a twelve-year imprisonment.

The Earliest Baptist Church in Wales: Above are the remains from the earliest Baptist church in Wales—located in Ilston and established in 1649. Not long after its beginning, the church relocated to the nearby town of Swansea, Wales. Pictured on the opposite page is the Bethseda Baptist Chapel that stands today in Swansea.

Bunyan was initially sentenced to three-months' imprisonment under the "Conventicle Act." This obscure English law from 1592 made attendance in the Established Church compulsory and imprisoned anyone who did not attend or persuaded others to not attend. (Holding a nonconformist church service was obviously influencing others to not attend the Church of England.) The penalty was three-months' imprisonment and a promise not to reoffend. Repeat offenders would be banished from England and, if they returned, executed.

Thus every three months, Bunyan had the opportunity to be released to his family if he would only promise to quit preaching. He refused: "I have determined, the Almighty God being my help and shield, yet to suffer, if frail life might continue so long, even till the moss shall grow on mine eyebrows, rather than thus to violate my faith and principles."[7]

Bunyan's wife Elizabeth remained faithful to the Lord in her husband's absence. The couple, who had been married just under two years, were expecting their first child together when he was arrested. Due to the strain of his arrest, she went into labor and miscarried.

In the coming months, Elizabeth valiantly worked to secure his release. A well-known story told of her appearing before a panel of judges in London bears repeating here.

After the judges had made a variety of excuses for why Bunyan could not be released, one of them finally asked the only question they all cared about:

"Would he leave off preaching?"

"My lord," said she, "he dares not leave preaching as long as he can speak."

What, then, was the use of talking about him? asked Twisdon, to which she made reply that her husband simply desired to live peaceably and to follow his calling, and so maintain his family.

"There is need for this, my lord," adds she, "for I have four small children that cannot help themselves, of which one is blind, and we have nothing to live upon but the charity of good people."

"Hast thou four children?" asked Sir Matthew Hale, pitifully. "Thou art but a young woman to have four children."

"My lord," replied she, "I am but mother-in-law [stepmother] to them, having not been married to him yet full two years. Indeed, I was with child when my husband was first apprehended; but being young and unaccustomed to such things, I being smayed at the news, fell into labor, and so continued for eight days, and then was delivered; but my child died."

Sir Matthew, feeling the pathos of this touching story, exclaimed, "Alas, poor woman!"

But Twisdon, a man of quite another mould, rudely repelled her, and told her plainly that she made poverty her cloak, and that, as he understood, her husband found it a much better thing to run up and down preaching than to follow his calling [occupation].

"What is his calling?" asked Sir Matthew, to which a chorus of voices replied, "A tinker, my lord!"

"Yes," said the dauntless woman, "and because he is a tinker and a poor man, therefore he is despised and cannot have justice."

The conversation continued back and forth similarly until Judge Chester lost patience.

He grew more angry, and said, "My lord, he [Bunyan] will preach and do what he lists [wants]!"

But, replied she, "He preacheth nothing but the word of God!"

Twisdon, too, irritated both at the persistent woman and his more lenient colleague, went into a great rage.

Elizabeth told her husband afterwards that she thought he would have struck her.[8]

Brave woman indeed.

Bunyan wrote of the agony of leaving his family. Not only was the separation painful to him, but, as Elizabeth had stated to the judges, they were very poor, and he was concerned for their well being. He wrote while in prison:

> The parting with my wife and poor children, hath often been to me in this place, as the pulling the flesh from the bones; and also it brought to my mind the many hardships, miseries, and wants that my poor family was like to meet with, should I be taken from them, especially my poor blind child, who lay nearer my heart than all beside: Oh! the thoughts of the hardships I thought my poor blind one might go under, would break my heart to pieces.[9]

The prison itself, which stands on the corner of High Street and Silver Street, had little light and no bathing facilities. It was often overcrowded and the stench must have been revolting. Typhus fever was a constant danger and claimed the lives of many prisoners.

In prison, Bunyan made shoelaces, which a friend sold for him, to help support his family. He had his Bible, a copy of *Foxe's Book of Martyrs*, and some writing materials. He continued his prolific writing ministry, writing at least nine books, possibly including part one of *Pilgrim's Progress*, during this time in prison.

Prison Door: The prison where John Bunyan was held has been rebuilt since the seventeenth century. This original door, however, is kept in the John Bunyan Museum in Bedford.

Bunyan also stayed in touch with his church family (some of whom were periodically imprisoned with him) and, upon the death of Pastor Gifford and while still in prison, Bunyan was asked to be their pastor. Surprisingly, he also had occasional opportunities to meet with other Christians and to preach outside of the prison, thanks to a sympathetic jailer who trusted Bunyan's promise to return. These opportunities apparently came to an end when Bunyan was spotted in London while still supposedly in prison.

But even within the prison, Bunyan had many opportunities to preach. He thanked the Lord for giving him "freedom" in prison to study Scripture, pray, sing, write, and hold services for the other prisoners, which often included fellow nonconformists. His preaching even drew hearers from outside, as people would gather around the prison to hear as he projected his voice and proclaimed his message.

In March of 1672, King Charles II issued the Declaration of Indulgence, which suspended charges and penalties against religious prisoners. Bunyan was released in May of that year—and immediately resumed preaching.

Bedford Church: The nonconformist church that John Bunyan pastored remains an independent church to this day.

• • • • •

For the next sixteen years, Bunyan continued to pastor, preach, and write. His popularity grew, and although he traveled much to preach, he remained committed to serving the flock at Bedford rather than accepting opportunities for larger churches in larger cities. His preaching and writing were not only full of Scripture but were seasoned by suffering, which perhaps partially explains their entrance into so many hearts.

Bunyan suffered one more imprisonment—much shorter this time, as it was only six months—from the fall to spring of 1675–76. (He may have written part two of *Pilgrim's Progress* during this time.) But although he was only arrested once, he was never far from the possibility of it. These were tense days in England for nonconformists and anyone else not part of the Church of England. Across the country, church services were disrupted and Christians taken to prison, including Bunyan's friends

Grave at Bunhill Fields: The monument over Bunyan's tomb was erected in 1862 and depicts scenes from *Pilgrim's Progress.*

in ministry.[10] Bunyan himself gives us a glimpse into the strain of those years in his book *Israel's Hope Encouraged*: "Our days indeed have been days of trouble, especially since the discovery of the Popish plot, for then we began to fear cutting of throats, of being burned in our beds, and of seeing our children dashed in pieces before our faces."[11] Through it all, however, Bunyan continued to preach, exercising caution when he could and boldness at all times.

John and Elizabeth remained married until his death in 1688. Theirs was a marriage of spiritual union and mutual love not always evident in this time period in England. In addition to the four children from John's first marriage, they had two more together—a daughter and a son.

Pilgrim's Progress was published in 1678 and became an immediate bestseller. It seems, however, that it brought more gain to its publisher than to its author as Bunyan remained a man of poor-to-modest means his entire life. His generosity may have also played a part in his continuing poverty.

In 1688, as Bunyan rode by horseback to a preaching engagement in London, he made a sixty-mile detour to Reading to help reconcile a father and a son. His efforts were successful, but as he then rode toward London, he was caught in a storm and fell ill with a fever. He died a few days later at his friend John Strudwick's house. Most likely, Elizabeth didn't know of his illness until after he died. Strudwick buried Bunyan in his own tomb at Bunhill Fields, the recently-opened nonconformist burial ground in London.

Bunyan's tomb today is the most prominent at Bunhill Fields, thanks to a statue placed over his grave in 1862, and his name is revered in England. In his lifetime, however, he had every reason to consider himself only a pilgrim who served his Lord either in prison or living at its threshold.

Bunyan, like those in Hebrews 11, held fast to God's promises "and confessed that they were strangers and pilgrims on the earth. For they that say such things declare plainly that they seek a country. And truly, if they had been mindful of that country from whence they came out, they might have had opportunity to have returned. But now they desire a better country, that is, an heavenly . . . " (Hebrews 11:13–16). What joy must have been his as he finished his pilgrim journey and entered the Celestial City!

TRUTHS FOR OUTSIDERS

What do we learn from the life of John Bunyan?

God's grace is greater than our sin. I love the title of Bunyan's autobiography: *Grace Abounding to the Chief of Sinners.* It is, of course, a reference to both Romans 5:20 and 1 Timothy 1:15: "But where sin abounded, grace did much more abound" and "Christ Jesus came into the world to save sinners; of whom I am chief."

But it's not just John Bunyan or the Apostle Paul—all of us have great reason to be thankful that God's grace far exceeds our sin. We never outgrow grace, and we need never despair of its availability.

God's grace is sufficient through suffering. In addition to the physical suffering of being in prison, Bunyan faced a peculiar level of psychological suffering as well. Although he was in prison for twelve years, he was never sentenced for any more than three months at a time. While he remained willing to suffer as long as God saw fit, it must have been tantalizing to be continually wondering if and when there might be a political shift that would change the laws or a sympathetic judge who would have him released. And then, even after his release, the final sixteen years of Bunyan's ministry were also spent under the threat of likely rearrest.

Through all of this, God's grace was sufficient—not just for the day-to-day difficulty, but also for the accumulated strain of an uncertain future. In 1684, he wrote a book titled *Seasonable Counsel, or Advice to Sufferers* which is built around a text he surely had claimed many times: "Wherefore let them that suffer according to the will of God commit the keeping of their souls to him in well doing, as unto a faithful Creator" (1 Peter 4:19).

God has a purpose in our suffering. I don't think *Pilgrim's Progress* would have nearly the impact God has given it had it been written from the comforts of a pastor's study. George Whitfield remarked that this book "smells of the prison." Unlike many of the books born in the midst of twenty-first century western prosperity and freedom, *Pilgrim's Progress* portrays the Christian life as one with suffering woven through it. Bunyan *expected* suffering. And he discovered that God has a purpose in the midst of our pain.

If you are in a season of suffering, don't be surprised. And don't assume God is doing nothing just because you cannot see how He is working. God may be bringing the greatest good you'll ever know from this very season. "And we know that all things work together for good to them that love God, to them who are the called according to his purpose. For whom he did foreknow, he also did predestinate to be conformed to the image of his Son . . ." (Romans 8:28–29).

Preaching is a non-negotiable tenant of New Testament Christianity. Sometimes in the larger picture of Bunyan's experience of suffering we forget that he could have ended it at any three-month interval had he simply promised to never preach again. The fact that he endured twelve years of prison specifically because of his commitment to preach is a testimony to the high esteem with which he regarded preaching.

Many today downplay the importance of preaching, replacing it with apologetics or Bible teaching. Both of these have their place, but there can be no replacement for preaching. Paul also highly esteemed preaching. In 1 Corinthians 1:21 he wrote, "For after that in the wisdom of God the world by wisdom knew not God, it pleased God by the foolishness of preaching to save them that believe."

If you are a preacher, I encourage you to not take your calling lightly. And if you are not a preacher, I encourage you, too, to place a priority on preaching by being present to hear it and attentive to apply it to your life.

JOHN NEWTON
(1725–1807)

"I am not what I ought to be, I am not what I wish to be, I am not what I hope to be. But I thank God I am not what I once was, and I can say with the great apostle, 'By the grace of God I am what I am.'"

John Newton

If you have the chance to visit London for a few days, you should spend at least half a day in Olney. It's a quaint English town in its own right, but its connection to history is why I love it.

Just sixty miles north of London proper, Olney is the city where both John Newton and William Cowper lived for almost two decades. You can visit Cowper's home, which has been made into a Newton-Cowper museum, as well as visit Newton's church and see the pulpit from which he preached over two centuries ago.

In the cemetery next to the church, you can visit the gravesite of Newton and his wife Mary. The epitaph on Newton's tombstone, which he wrote before he died, is in itself a mini biography of his life:

John Newton, clerk, once an infidel and libertine, a servant of slaves in Africa, was by the rich mercy of our Lord and Saviour Jesus Christ, preserved, restored, pardoned, and appointed to preach the faith he had long labored to destroy.

I suppose most American Christians are aware that John Newton penned the words to what is perhaps the most-sung hymn in the English language, "Amazing Grace." Some may be aware of a few snapshots of Newton's life. But I doubt many are familiar with the larger picture and just how remarkably God displayed His grace to and through this man.

• • • • •

John Newton was born in London in 1725. His father, John Newton Sr., was a successful sea captain who was often away on trading voyages. But his mother, Elizabeth, was a faithful nonconformist Christian who diligently sought to instill God's Word in young John's heart. She helped him commit to memory large passages of Scripture and many hymns. God would use these stored up truths in his life in years to come.

Newton was an only child, and Elizabeth, with her husband often gone, devoted herself to teaching her son academically as well as spiritually. He was a quick learner, and by the time John was four years old, she had taught him to read. By the time he was six, she was teaching him Latin.

Thirteen days before Newton's seventh birthday, however, his mother died of tuberculosis. He was beside himself with grief. When his father returned from sea a year later, he remarried and sent John to a boarding school for what would turn out to be John's only two years of formal education.

In 1736, when Newton was eleven years old, his father took him to sea with him. Over the next six years, Newton made six voyages across the Mediterranean as cabin boy on his father's ship. From his father, he learned the skills of a sailor. From the other sailors, he learned the ways of unsaved men. From books and his companions onboard, he learned the doubts of an agnostic.

When Newton was seventeen years old, his father, recently retired, arranged an opportunity for him to work on a sugar plantation in Jamaica, which would have set John up for a prosperous livelihood. Days before his ship was to sail, his father sent him on a quick, three-day errand to Kent, England. While there, John visited the Catlett family who had been close friends of his mother. He intended to stay only briefly, but the moment he saw their daughter, Mary, he fell in love. Mary, being four years younger than Newton, was too young to even consider marriage, but he was so enchanted by her that he overstayed his visit three weeks, purposefully missing the departure of the ship on which he had been set to sail to Jamaica.

The Church Where John Newton Pastored in Olney: Located on the edge of town, it provides a pastoral scene that mirrors his care for the flock in Olney.

The irresponsibility, lack of discipline, and disregard for (if not blatant rebellion toward) authority evident in this incident was typical of young Newton and would only become more pronounced in the years ahead. In God's divine providence, however, He used Newton's love for Mary, immature and reckless as it may have been, as a preserver and restraint in his life in the years ahead.

John Newton's Pulpit: Although not used on a weekly basis, John Newton's pulpit can still be viewed inside his church.

Newton's father, angry and frustrated, found a place for Newton on a ship as a crew member. Newton sailed to Venice and back, and it was on this trip that he completely cast off any remaining belief in God and declared himself an infidel. Perhaps not coincidentally, he also cast off restraints of virtue and morals at the same time. Still, he thought of and planned to marry Mary Catlett.

When Newton returned from this voyage, he went down to the docks looking for new employment one evening where he was captured and forcibly impressed into the Royal Navy on board the *HMS Harwich*. Newton's father was not able to get him released, but he was able to get Newton promoted to midshipman.

While at sea, Newton became known for his blasphemous language and, as he described on his tombstone, *libertine* (lacking moral restraint) ways. Deeply resentful of the delay that being impressed into the navy had made to his plans to propose to Mary, he made an attempted desertion. When he was captured and returned to the ship, his punishment was severe—eight dozen lashes with the entire crew watching as well as being degraded to the rank of a common sailor.

Newton's near-death flogging and terrible humiliation turned his resentment at his circumstances to seething hatred toward the captain. At one point, he even planned to murder the captain and commit suicide after, but thoughts of Mary and dreams of a future life with her restrained him.

Sometime later, as the *Harwich* was en route to India, they passed the *Pegasus*, a slaving ship bound for Africa. Newton requested and was granted a transfer.

On the *Pegasus*, Newton returned to the worst of his ways and brought much of the crew down with him. He openly mocked the captain and purposefully stirred up trouble. When they reached the Plantanes, a set of three islands off the coast of Sierra Leone, West Africa, the captain died, and his first mate who deemed Newton as nothing but trouble, left him behind with a European slave dealer, Amos Clowe.

Newton's troubles were only beginning.

· · · · ·

If you or I had met Newton at this point in his life and perhaps tried sharing the gospel with him, I'm afraid we would have thought of him as a hardened sinner who, having cast aside God's repeated opportunities for mercy, was beyond hope. But God saw beyond Newton's present and his exterior, and He allowed further humiliation and pain to bring him to a point of seeing his need for the God he delighted in blaspheming.

Clowe's native wife, Pi, took an instant disliking to Newton. When Newton came down with jungle fever and Clowe left him behind as he made a trip to another island, Pi began to treat him as her slave, cruelly withholding not only medical care, but basic necessities such as food and shelter. Under the burning African sun, Newton reeled in and out of consciousness. Amazingly, he pulled through. When he began to recover from the fever, however, Pi made him perform menial and useless tasks, mocking him as he did them in his tattered clothes and weakened condition. Newton became the lowest slave on the island so that even Pi's native slaves pitied him and would occasionally try to sneak food from their own meager portions to him without Pi's knowledge. It is this period of his life to which he referred on his tombstone as "a servant of slaves in Africa."

Newton began to sink into despair—not a despair leading to repentance, but a human breaking down of the will. One thing kept him going, however—the hope of seeing Mary again.

Meanwhile, back in England, Newton's father was deeply concerned for his son. He asked a merchant captain friend to find him, sparing no expense, and bring him back to England.

Considering the vast expanses of even the *coast* of Africa, this mission to find Newton was something like looking for a needle in a haystack. And, outside of the providence of God, it would not have happened.

As it was, Newton, who was now working for another trader on the interior of the island, made a trip to the coast one day on business. He had planned to go two days earlier but had been delayed. As he conducted his business, his companion went to the beach to look for any passing ships he might flag down to which they could sell the items they had brought with them. A ship, which just happened to be captained by the very man Newton's father had sent to look for him, was nearby. One half hour later, it would have been gone. Newton's friend went out in a canoe to sell wares, and the captain asked if he had ever heard of an Englishman named John Newton.

A few hours later, Newton was aboard the *Greyhound*, homeward bound. But he didn't pause once to consider the miraculous deliverance God had just given him.

For the first time in his life, Newton was merely a passenger aboard a ship, not a crewman. If he had been a poor influence on sailors when he was one of them, he was even worse when he had nothing but time on his hands. With the pressures of his life lifted, he immediately reverted to his old ways and often drew the crew into drunken, blasphemous nights of revelry. Additionally, he aggressively sought to convert them to his infidel beliefs. The captain began to refer to Newton as a Jonah and rue the day he had brought him on board.

One day, however, Newton picked up a copy of Thomas Aquinas' *The Imitation of Christ* simply to pass time. As he read, involuntary thoughts came to him in the form of questions: *What if this is true? What if my mother's faith was real? What if it isn't that I've* disproved *the existence of God, but that I simply have not experienced it?* Disturbed by these thoughts, he closed the book and went to bed.

But God wasn't done with Newton. That night, he was awakened by a violent storm and water pouring into his cabin.

All night long, Newton helped the others pump water while the storm raged and water filled their boat faster than they could pump it out. The fact that their primary cargo was beeswax and camwood—both lighter than water—helped keep the ship afloat.

Finally, morning broke and the storm abated a little. The men used their clothing and bedding to plug up the largest holes on the ship, nailing them in with boards. About 9:00 that morning, as Newton finished discussing their continued efforts at pumping water with the captain, he turned to leave and heard himself say, "If this will not do, the Lord have mercy on us." As he walked away, he realized what he had just said. It was the first time in years that he had used God's name in any way besides a curse word or that he had considered even the idea of mercy.

As Newton returned to pump, the Scriptures he had memorized with his mother flooded his mind. For the first time in years, he saw himself as a sinner justly deserving God's wrath and desperately needing God's mercy.

The storm returned with vengeance, and for the next eleven days, it continued. On the afternoon of March 21, Newton, physically unable to continue pumping, was assigned to take the wheel, keeping the ship pointed into the storm to keep her from capsizing.

Once again alone with his thoughts, he began to see God's extraordinary hand of providence over the past few years of his life, and the Holy Spirit worked a deep sense of conviction over his sin. He remembered what his mother had told him of Christ and His substitutionary death on the cross. His infidel beliefs began to weaken, and he suddenly wanted to know if the gospel really *was* true.

That evening, the storm ended and the men were able to pump out the last of the water. Newton found the captain's Bible and began reading it—not to mock it, but to know the truth.

Although it would be some months before he made a definite decision to place his faith in Christ, this moment was the turning point. In fact, fifty-seven years later (when Newton was eighty years old), he remembered the day in his journal: "March 21, 1805. Not well able to write. But I endeavor to observe the return of this day with Humiliation, Prayer, and Praise."[1] When Newton wrote his autobiography, he titled it *Out of the Depths*, a phrase from the Psalm: "Out of the depths have I cried unto thee, O LORD ... there is forgiveness with thee" (Psalm 130:1, 4).

Newton had sunk low, but God's grace reached lower. He, once a libertine and infidel, had been preserved, restored, pardoned.

• • • • •

Due to Newton's complete change of behavior after his conversion on the *Greyhound*, he was able to find work as a first mate on a slave ship that would soon depart for Africa, in view of a later position as captain, with a friend of his father's.

Years later, Newton deeply regretted his three voyages (this one and two more as captain) in the slave trade. In his later years, he used his own testimony to make England aware of the horrors of this human trafficking and greatly helped the abolition movement. In his twenties, however, he simply accepted the slave trade as a fact of life and thought himself kind for giving more humane treatment to the slaves on his ship.

In between Newton's first and second voyages, he proposed to Mary, she accepted, and they married quickly before Newton departed for the sea again. Two days before Newton was to set sail on his fourth voyage, he was having tea with his wife when he was suddenly taken in a seizure that lasted about an hour. When the seizure passed, he was weak and dizzy, and his doctor advised he not sail again.

Grateful to no longer be separated from Mary, Newton found work as a tide surveyor. The position paid well and required little time—a perfect combination for Newton to begin serious Bible study. He read the Bible many times through as well as any other Christian book recommended to him. He even undertook the study of Hebrew and Greek.

William Cowper's Summer House: This tiny house in the garden is where Cowper did much of his writing.

During this time, Newton's mother's prayers from three decades earlier were answered as he began to sense a call to preach.

In 1758, Newton applied for ordination. At the time, he was refused, based on his past ungodly lifestyle. But a few years later, he began receiving invitations from churches to share his remarkable testimony. Through these opportunities, and with now several years of a faithful Christian testimony, his call to preach became apparent to all. Finally, in 1764, he was offered a pastorate in Olney, England, and began the most fruitful years of his life, "appointed to preach the faith he had long labored to destroy."

● ● ● ● ●

As you drive into Olney today, there is a sign that reads, "Welcome to Olney, home of Amazing Grace." But when John and Mary Newton first arrived, it was only a poor town with a church in need of a pastor.

The church is on the south side of town, and partially surrounding it are sheep pastures, protected by stone walls. It's a hallmark-card scene that pictures the pastoral care Newton gave his beloved flock into which he and Mary poured their lives. Newton's preaching was so popular that the church added an inside gallery to seat more listeners.

Early on, Newton began a Thursday afternoon class for children—something like our Sunday schools today. He personally taught the two hundred children who attended weekly.

It was also at Olney where Newton befriended William Cowper, an extraordinarily gifted poet who struggled with extreme depression.

The lives of Newton and Cowper were so connected in Olney that William Cowper's house has been turned into The Cowper and Newton Museum. It's a fascinating place to spend a couple hours. Each room is filled with original pieces of furniture that one or the other of them used as well as historical artifacts and information on both of their lives.

Cowper's own testimony is full of God's amazing grace and providence.

• • • • •

William Cowper was born in 1731, making him just six years younger than Newton. Like Newton, his mother died when he was six. Also like Newton, he was sent to a boarding school shortly after.

From his earliest years, Cowper had the soul of an artist, almost to the point of a stereotype. He was sensitive, bookish, thoughtful, and timid. God would greatly use these traits in the future. But in boarding school, they made him particularly vulnerable to being bullied, including in the most personal and invasive ways.

On the academic front, however, Cowper excelled. During these years in school, he developed a love for poetry, read through some of the great literary classics, and learned Latin well enough to compose original poetry in it.

Whether triggered by his experiences in boarding school or a unique physiological mental illness, Cowper suffered complete mental breakdowns including periods of insanity throughout his life. The first came in 1763 as he was studying for a law examination. After three attempts at suicide, he was committed to an asylum.

At the asylum, Cowper was treated by a Christian doctor who shared the gospel with him on multiple occasions. One day as Cowper was walking through a hallway, he picked up a Bible lying on a chair by the window and happened to read these words in Romans 3:24–25: "Being justified freely by his grace through the redemption that is in Christ Jesus: Whom God hath set forth to be a propitiation through faith in his blood, to declare his righteousness for the remission of sins that are past, through the forbearance of God."

The reality of Christ's substitutionary death for his sins broke through to him, and he placed his faith in Jesus. He later described the moment: "Immediately I received strength to believe it, and the full beams of the Sun of Righteousness shone upon me. I saw the sufficiency of the atonement that he had made, my pardon sealed in his blood, and all the fulness and completeness of his justification. In a moment I believed, and received the gospel."[2]

Cowper was a new man. The depression which he had struggled with all of his adult life did not vanish upon his salvation. In fact, he eventually suffered two more complete breakdowns. But he now had the spiritual realities of the gospel with which to combat his seasons of melancholy. And foundational to his growth in God's grace and understanding of Bible truth was his relationship with John Newton.

Shortly after Cowper's salvation, he moved to Olney. The garden behind Cowper's house in Olney (which you can walk through when you visit his home) joined to the orchard behind Newton's back yard. John and Mary Newton befriended their new neighbor, and Cowper benefited greatly from their spiritual encouragement. He began attending Newton's church.

As a poet, Cowper profoundly influenced English literature and reshaped modern poetry. His most famous secular works include his translation of the *Illiad and Odyssey* from the Greek originals. His poetry was unique in that its subject matter was often common, everyday objects or routines, from which he drew either humor or a descriptive angle with which readers could relate.

One of the gifts that God gave Cowper through his sensitive temperament and perhaps even through his mental illness was a brilliant and poetic clarity during his healthy seasons. It may be that the sun shown brighter in the mind of this poet who had so personally experienced the darkness.

Seeing Cowper's gift for poetry and wanting to encourage his spiritual growth as well as direct his thoughts toward scriptural comfort, Newton invited him to help with a hymnal he was writing. It was for this project that Cowper wrote the hymn "There Is a Fountain Filled with Blood"—a glad song of praise for his salvation. He also wrote "God Moves in a Mysterious Way" (originally titled "Light Shining out of Darkness") for this project.

The book was published in 1779 as *Olney Hymns* and contained 68 hymns by Cowper and 280 by Newton. Newton's contributions included "Glorious Things of Thee Are Spoken" and, of course, "Faith's Great Aim and Expectation," which we know today as "Amazing Grace."

John Newton's Chair: This chair stood in the study at Newton's house in Olney where he wrote "Amazing Grace."

Cowper suffered two more mental breakdowns in Olney. During the first, Newton and Mary invited Cowper to their home for several months. They tenderly cared for and encouraged him during this season of debilitating depression.

Four years before Cowper's death in 1800, he suffered another breakdown, from which he never recovered. By this time, Newton had moved to London, but he faithfully wrote Cowper and visited him occasionally.[3] A letter which Cowper wrote Newton after one of these visits in 1788 gives insight into their relationship as well as the pastoral heart of Newton:

> I found those comforts in your visit, which have formerly sweetened all our interviews, in part restored. I knew you; knew you for the same

shepherd who was sent to lead me out of the wilderness into the pasture where the Chief Shepherd feeds his flock, and felt my sentiments of affectionate friendship for you the same as ever. But one thing was still wanting, and that the crown of all. I shall find it in God's time, if it be not lost forever.[4]

The last two sentences reference the spiritual despondency Cowper struggled with during this season, believing he could not be a true Christian. Yet, when Newton conducted Cowper's funeral a couple years later, he pointed out that Cowper, whose face had lit into an expression of wonder and delight as he died, was at that moment in the presence of Christ with every cloud of depression dissipated.

• • • • •

Sixteen years after Newton's arrival in Olney, St. Mary Church of Woolnoth, London, called him as their pastor, and he accepted. Newton pastored his church in London for the next twenty-eight years with the same tender love, careful study, and Scripture-filled preaching with which he had shepherded Olney.

It was in London where Newton became a personal friend and encourager of William Wilberforce, Hannah More, Charles Simeon, Henry Martyn, William Carey, John Wesley, George Whitfield, and several other people whose names we still remember.[5]

His friendship with Wilberforce, in particular, was important, because it was through Newton that Wilberforce first heard the gospel as a child. And when he trusted Christ years later as a young adult, he went to Newton for counsel on if he should pursue his political aspirations. Newton encouraged him to use his political platform to fight slavery, and Newton himself helped by writing pamphlets for the abolition movement.

Newton also asked Cowper to help with poetry, which he did. Cowper's most famous on this subject was titled "The Negro's Complaint," which looks at slavery from the perspective of a slave and became a powerful, heart-reaching tool for abolitionists.

Newton continued to speak out against slavery publicly and to encourage Wilberforce personally. In 1788, Newton even testified before the Prime Minister William Pitt's Privy Council on the horrors of the slave trade which he had seen first hand. He rejoiced to see the Slave Trade Act of 1807 passed.

Another aspect of Newton's personal ministry and his relationship with Wilberforce, of which I was unaware until recently, was his influence to send the gospel to England's new colony of Australia in 1788. As you may remember, the first settlers Great Britain sent to Australia were convicts. But as that "First Fleet" of eleven ships arrived in Botany Bay in 1788, it not only carried 750 convicts and 213 marines sent to escort them, but it also carried a man and his wife—Richard and Mary Johnson—who went at the special invitation of Newton to preach the gospel and establish a church.

Months previously, when Newton heard of the prisoners who would be sailing to Australia, he immediately felt concern that a chaplain should be sent with them. Not only did he and Wilberforce together influence Prime Minister William Pitt to send such a chaplain, but Newton personally asked his friend, thirty-one-year-old Johnson, if he would pray about going as a missionary to Australia. One biographer records of Newton's invitation to Johnson: "Newton was crystal clear about the cost involved to embark on such a grand journey, and the call required to undertake such a glorious mission. He wrote: 'A minister who should go to Botany Bay without a call from the Lord, and without receiving

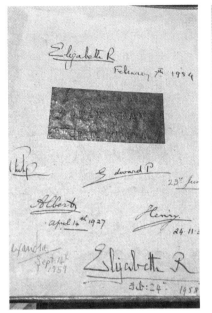

First Bible Sent to Australia: This Bible, kept at St. Philip's Church in Sydney, is inscribed "Botany Bay, 1786" and was sent with the First Fleet that arrived in Australia in 1788. It was later signed by Queen Elizabeth and other members of the Royal Family.

from Him an apostolic spirit, the spirit of a missionary, enabling him to forsake all, to give up all, to venture all, to put himself into the Lord's hands without reserve, to sink or swim, had better run his head against a brick wall.'"[8]

Johnson did go, and God greatly used him. For four years he held services in the open air waiting for a church building the government had promised. Finally, tired of waiting, Johnson built a church himself. Throughout the week, he and his wife Mary conducted a school for nearly two hundred children.

And Newton didn't forget Johnson once he had left, but he continued to pray for and write him. During one particularly discouraging season in Johnson's ministry, Newton wrote him:

I have not been disheartened by your apparent want of success. I have been told that skillful gardeners will undertake to sow and raise a salad for dinner in the short time while the meat is roasting. But no gardener can raise oaks with such expedition. You are sent to New Holland, not to sow salad seeds, but to plant acorns; and your labor will not be lost, though the first appearances may be very small, and the progress very slow. You are, I trust, planting for the next century. I have a good hope that your oaks will one day spring up and flourish, and produce other acorns, which, in due time, will take root, and spread among the islands and nations in the Southern Ocean.[9]

Johnson's labor did bear fruit into the next century . . . and the next. The spread of the gospel throughout Australia traces back to Richard and Mary Johnson, and before them to the pastor in London who cared about the souls of the convicts being sent off to a far-away land.

· · · · ·

Newton was faithful to the end—faithful to His Saviour, faithful to his wife (Mary died in 1790; theirs had been a tender, godly marriage), faithful to his church, and faithful to the gospel.

As Newton neared his eightieth birthday, a friend suggested he should retire. "What!" he responded, "Shall the old African blasphemer stop while he can speak?" In his final years, Newton began losing his eyesight, and then his hearing. But still, he continued preaching until the final months of his life when he was no longer physically able.

One month before he died, Newton remarked, "It is a great thing to die; and, when flesh and heart fail, to have God for the strength of our heart, and our portion forever. I know whom I have believed, and he is able to keep that which I have committed against that great day.

Henceforth there is laid up for me a crown of righteousness, which the Lord, the righteous Judge, shall give me that day."

Hours before his death, he said, "My memory is nearly gone, but I remember two things: that I am a great sinner and that Christ is a great Saviour."[10]

It has been over two hundred years since December 21, 1807, when Newton entered the presence of Jesus, yet he still has no less days to sing God's praise than when he first begun.

TRUTHS FOR OUTSIDERS

What do we learn from the life of John Newton?

Don't give up praying for those who have resisted God's grace. Who knows to what extent Newton's salvation was the answer to his godly mother's prayers? Newton himself believed this to be the case. If you have an unsaved loved one who has resisted the gospel and spurned God's grace, don't give up praying for them. Even during the times that Newton was most vigorously rejecting Christ, God was providentially working situations in his life to give him further opportunities to turn to Christ.

God's amazing grace can bring good even out of our sinful past. One of the blessings in reading Newton's autobiography is that he was careful to magnify God's grace rather than his sinful past, including his participation in the slave trade after his salvation. Although Newton deeply regretted his voyages in the slave trade, God allowed him to use even these experiences to help end the blight of slavery in England.

Christian friendship can lighten a heavy load. Newton's friendship to Cowper helped birth hymns such as "There Is a Fountain Filled with Blood," which has blessed countless Christians and has been instrumental in leading unbelievers to Christ. But even if Cowper had never written this hymn, Newton's kindness and friendship lightened his suffering in marked ways. We can learn from Newton to be purposeful in encouraging those who suffer with depression and despair.

Rejoice in God's providence. What besides the providence of God would have brought Cowper to the Newtons' backyard? And it wasn't just for Cowper, and it wasn't just for Newton. This God-ordained meeting brought far-reaching encouragement to us today through the testimonies and hymns published by these neighbors.

Persevere through seasons of difficulty. Both Newton and Cowper had seasons of suffering in their lives. Perhaps the most painful for Newton was Mary's death, and the most difficult for Cowper was ongoing mental illness. For both of them, however, there were blessings on the other side of their suffering. Had Cowper given up in despair, he, not to mention we, would have missed the rich hymns he later wrote. Had Newton given up, his flock in London would have lost their dear pastor. Don't give up.

Thank God for His grace. Every blessing, victory, and spiritual fruit in our lives is a result of God's grace. Remain amazed at its far-reaching abundance in your life.

WILLIAM CAREY
(1761–1834)

"Expect great things from God; attempt great things for God."

William Carey

I f you were to choose someone to reshape the attitude and methods toward missions of an entire generation of Christians, what kind of person would you seek out? An astute PhD with published studies on leading change? Or perhaps someone more hands-on— a worldwide traveler who has experienced and understood a wide variety of cultures? Maybe a Bible scholar with evangelistic pulpit skills to convince congregations of their responsibility to the lost?

None of these describe the person God chose.

William Carey, to whom we refer today as "the father of modern missions," was a poor shoe cobbler who could boast only a short formal education, had never traveled outside of his and the neighboring county, and miserably failed at his first sermon.

But God developed within Carey something no one else he knew had—a heart for lost souls around the world. This burden consumed him and compelled him to challenge the complacency of his generation—first with words, and then with example and fruit to the glory of God.

• • • • •

William Carey was born on August 17, 1761, in Paulerspury, Northamptonshire, England—just fifteen miles from Olney. Carey's parents, Edmund and Elizabeth, were weavers, and he was the oldest of five children. Edmond was also the schoolmaster for the small village grammar school, which Carey attended until he was twelve years old.

Even at a young age, Carey was intellectually inquisitive. His insatiable love for learning motivated him to teach himself Latin, botany, and geography. His seemingly incessant talk of exploration earned him the nickname "Columbus" among his friends.

Shoe Sign: This sign reads "Second Hand Shoes Bought and Sold" and hung at Carey's cobbler shop.

When Carey turned fourteen, his parents apprenticed him to Clarke Nichols, a shoemaker in nearby Piddington, who, like Carey's parents, attended the Church of England. At that time in England (much as is the case today), the Established Church had both an evangelical group of churches and a more traditionally Anglican high-church group. The traditional group emphasized sacraments, liturgy, and outward forms of religion, all which resulted in a tendency to obscure the gospel. The evangelical group emphasized the necessity of salvation by faith in Christ. (John Newton, who stayed with the Established Church, was known as one of the only two evangelical pastors in London during the time he pastored there.) Neither the church Carey attended as a child nor the church Nichols attended was evangelistic, and Carey had never heard the simple, straightforward gospel.

Nichols, however, had another apprentice by the name of John Warr, who was a nonconformist, born-again Christian. Warr cared deeply about Carey's salvation and talked often with Carey about spiritual things as well as invited Carey to the church he attended. It took time, but finally the realities of the gospel broke through to Carey, and on February 10, 1779, at the age of seventeen, he placed his faith in Christ. No one around him could have had any idea how God would use the life of this new convert to send the gospel around the world.

Carey immediately became burdened for the salvation of his family and those around him. He joined Warr in witnessing to Nichols, and the two apprentices had the privilege of leading Nichols to Christ on his deathbed in 1779.

After Nichols' death, Carey found work with Thomas Old, another cobbler.[1] Old introduced Carey to his sister-in-law Dorthy Plackett, who, like many women in small eighteenth-century English villages, was illiterate. Unlikely as it seems, Carey with his unquenchable thirst for knowledge and Dorothy who could neither read nor write, married on June 10, 1781. Shortly after their marriage, Old died, and Carey took over his business.

* * * * *

Carey became a Baptist by conviction, which was by no means a thoughtless decision. Having been raised in the Church of England during a period in England's history in which there was great prejudice (and recent persecution) against dissenters, Carey was naturally wary of aligning himself with these outcasts. But it had been a dissenter, Warr, who had shown Carey the way of salvation, and Warr finally convinced Carey to attend church with him one Sunday.

At Carey's first service in Warr's church, Thomas Chater from Olney, a guest speaker, preached the sermon. The message was from Hebrews 13:13, "Let us go forth therefore unto him without the camp, bearing his reproach." Carey was amazed at the biblical depth of the message, the obvious reverence for God's Word and love for Christ, and the sound reasoning of Chater's applications. In that very first service, Carey was convinced that it was the dissenters who were "bearing His reproach," and he became one. From that day forward, Carey gladly identified as an outsider following Christ.

And Chater, for his part, recognized in Carey a true love for the Lord and took him under his wing. In June of 1782, Chater invited Carey to attend the association meeting of Particular Baptists in Olney, with leading pastors including John C. Ryland, Sr., Andrew Fuller, and John Sutcliff. All three of these men would become lifelong friends and future colaborers in gospel ministry.

Among other results, the meeting challenged Carey to carefully study Scripture regarding Baptist distinctives.[2] Through his study, he came to the conclusion that the New Testament taught baptism by immersion after salvation, and he presented himself for baptism to his new friend, Pastor John C. Ryland. He was baptized on October 5, 1783, in the River Nene. The next decade would prove to be perhaps the most formative in Carey's entire life.

• • • • •

By now, Carey was not only a cobbler, but he also ran a night school in his home to help make ends meet.

Ever the learner, Carey taught himself Hebrew, Italian, Dutch, and French while he made and mended shoes. He developed such a reputation for continued education that locals called his shop "Carey's College."

Even with all his duties and obligations, Carey cared deeply about the spiritual condition of people around him. A persistent soulwinner, even to his extended family, it was obvious to many that he would eventually be in vocational ministry.

But his entrance into ministry wasn't seamless. When two village churches—Moulton and Earls Barton—invited Carey to become their pastor, he turned to his friend John Sutcliff, pastor of Olney Baptist Church, for advice. Sutcliff invited Carey to join the church in Olney and put his call to ministry to the test by preaching for the congregation.

The trial sermon did not go well. The minute book of the church contains the record:

W. Carey, in consequence of a request from the Church, preached this evening. After which it was resolved that he . . . should engage again on suitable occasion for sometime before us, in order that further trial may be made of his ministerial Gifts.[3]

Terrie and I recently had the opportunity to visit this church in Olney, where Carey preached his first sermon, just down the street from John Newton's church. The pastor, Ian Field, graciously showed us around and gave his time to answer our many questions.

He related the story of Carey's first sermon and told us of the continuing mentoring role John Sutcliff had in Carey's life. Sutcliff encouraged Carey to remain in the church as a member for a year to receive instruction, and during this time Carey was afforded occasional opportunities to preach in surrounding village churches. Meanwhile, Sutcliff personally invested in discipling Carey and helping him develop pastoral gifts.

One year later, Carey again preached at Olney in view of ordination, and this time he was unanimously recommended by the congregation. One biographer relates that his ordination counsel consisting of "Ryland, who had baptized him; Sutcliff, who had commissioned him; and Fuller, who had recognized in him a greatness yet unfulfilled, together inducted him by prayer, preaching, and laying on of hands into his new office."[4]

(In years to come, Olney Baptist Church would remain

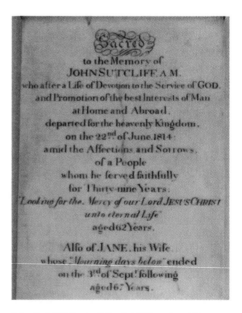

John Sutcliff: Pastor John Sutcliff mentored Carey in preaching. He is among those whom few people remember but shares in Carey's eternal spiritual fruit.

dear to Carey and he to them. It would be this church that prepared a sendoff service for his family when they went to India as missionaries, and it would also be this church that gave and sent a generous offering when his printing press burned in India.)

Carey was then called as the pastor at Moulton, but the church could pay him little, and he continued his work as a cobbler, in addition to his pastoral duties and his night school. Even so, he and Dorothy and the two young sons who had been born to them lived in grinding poverty. (Their first child had been a daughter, Ann, who died in infancy. The fever that claimed her life also brought Carey himself to death's door.)

Even with his time full in Moulton, Carey continued his self-education, studying church history and geography. Perhaps initially with his old boyhood desire for exploration, when the *Journal of Captain Cook's Last Voyage* had been published a few years earlier, Carey had read every word. But the book took Carey far beyond his boyhood desires. With a mind now changed by the gospel, he couldn't help but think of the people in these far-off lands who had never heard of Christ. He wrote later that this book "was the first thing that engaged my mind to think of missions."[5]

Carey began to study the Moravian missionaries of the seventeenth century who took the gospel to as far-off places as colonies in the New World, Africa, and the Far East. He had read about these places. He knew the languages they spoke, their history, and a few of their customs. He had imagined what it would be like to travel and live there. But why, he wondered, did he hear no one talk of taking the gospel to them *now*? Was it only for the previous century?

Ever searching, Carey obtained a copy of *David Brainerd's Journal*, published in 1749. Brainerd had been a missionary to the Native Americans and spent the final three years of his life in the wilderness of the American

Northeast, riding on horseback, sleeping in tents, and preaching the gospel even as tuberculosis steadily consumed his body. He died at the age of twenty-nine in the home of Jonathan Edwards, who obtained his permission to publish his journal after he died. (Henry Martyn, Adoniram Judson, and Jim Elliot were all also heavily influenced toward missions by *David Brainerd's Journal*.)

Carey read Brainerd's New Testament-soaked expressions of care for the unsaved Native Americans and of Brainerd's strenuous, sacrificial efforts to preach the gospel. As he read, he became convicted that the millions of people around the world with not so much as a gospel witness should cause great concern to every follower of Christ. Years later, he would plead, "Is not the commission of our Lord still binding upon us? Can we not do more than now we are doing?"

For now, however, he pondered. He read the New Testament. And he became convinced that it is the responsibility of every Bible-believing Christian to actively engage in taking the gospel around the world.

Carey pasted several sheets of paper together and made them into a map which he hung on the wall over his workbench. He scribbled in facts for nearly every country on the map, including its predominant religions and national population. As he studied the map, he considered and prayed for the people in China, Africa, India, the Caribbean Islands, and all the other places of which he had read who lived in spiritual darkness. He imagined faces. He prayed they might hear the gospel. And he wondered why no one did anything.

● ● ● ● ●

In 1786, at the pastor's annual association meeting, Carey put forth the question if it wasn't the church's responsibility to spread the gospel.

The Baptist churches in that association were steeped in what I would refer to as hyper-Calvinism. Believing that *election* in the Bible refers to God predetermining who will be saved and who will be lost, they carried that to its logical conclusion and assumed that their efforts had little influence in the matter.[6]

So when Carey put forth the question, his friend and mentor John Ryland, Sr. responded harshly, "Young man, sit down; when God is pleased to convert the heathen, He will do it without your help or mine."

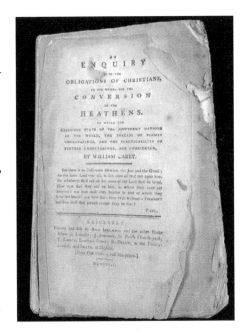

Copy of *An Enquiry*: This is a first edition copy of Carey's little book *An Enquiry*—a book that challenged churches across the English speaking world and became a manifesto for the modern missionary movement.

Carey sat down, but he didn't give up. He continued to study Scripture, witness to those around him, and plead with God to send missionaries to foreign lands to spread the gospel.

In 1792, Carey published *An Enquiry into the Obligations of Christians to Use Means for the Conversion of the Heathen*. This little book, which contained the data Carey had been collecting on his map as well as an impassioned plea for obedience to the Great Commission, became the manifesto for the modern missions movement.

The book was divided into five chapters, the titles of which give a glimpse into Carey's heart and the book's content:

Chapter 1: The Great Commission

Chapter 2: Earlier Missions

Chapter 3: A World Survey

Chapter 4: Can It Be Done?

Chapter 5: Our Duty

The response to this little book was encouraging. It even challenged Ryland, who began to have a change of heart toward missions. Over the next few years, Carey's book shook the Baptist churches in England out of complacency, and in the following decades, it did the same for churches in Europe and the New World.

At the Baptist association meeting on May 30, 1792, Carey preached what people today refer to as the "Deathless Sermon" because it included his now-famous quote, "Expect great things from God; attempt great things for God." The "great things" he called the pastors there to attempt was taking the gospel around the world.

Carey's listeners were stirred and began to leave with full minds and hearts. But Carey wasn't content to simply give people food for thought. He wanted something to be done. He pulled Andrew Fuller, who had shared Carey's burden for missions over the past few years, aside and said, "Are we not going to do anything? Oh Fuller, call them back, and let's do something in answer to God's call!"

Before the meeting's final dismissal, Fuller proposed that at the next meeting in a few months' time they definitely form a missionary society with the specific aim to send the gospel to another country. In October of 1792, The Particular Baptist Society for the Propagation of the Gospel amongst the Heathen (later shortened to the Baptist Missionary Society),

William Carey's Prayer Letters: Reading Carey's original prayer letters at Regent's Park College in the University of Oxford was a surreal experience.

had its first meeting. Among its charter members were William Carey, Andrew Fuller, John C. Ryland, Sr., and John Sutcliff.

Over the next six months, the newly-formed missionary organization raised funds to send two missionaries—veteran John Thomas and William Carey—to India.

Carey had not originally planned to be the missionary they sent. By now, he was a full-time pastor at Harvey Lane Baptist Church in Leicester. His church was not eager to lose their pastor, and he had the demands of a growing family. Dorothy was expecting their fourth child and was not inclined to go to a foreign country. It's not difficult to imagine the fears that she—a woman who had never been more than a few miles from her hometown and didn't share her husband's breadth of knowledge or, being illiterate, his ability to read and acclimate to new information—must have felt to consider going to a far-off land.

But as the weeks wore on and no one else volunteered to go with Thomas, Carey determined God would have him go. Fuller wrote of the meeting in which Carey presented himself: ". . . we saw there was a gold mine [of souls] in India, but it seemed almost as deep as the center of the earth. Who will venture to explore it? 'I will go down,' said Mr. Carey to his brethren, 'but remember that you must hold the ropes.' We solemnly engaged to do so; nor while we live, shall we desert him."

Carey and their oldest son, Felix, prepared to sail ahead, find suitable housing, and come back for Dorothy and the family. In the end, however, just hours before the ship was to sail, Carey managed to convince Dorothy to come, in part, because her sister Kitty was willing to come as well.

In April of 1793, less than one year after the "Deathless Sermon," the Carey family set sail to attempt great things for God in India. Carey would never see England again.

• • • • •

Carey's first years in India were brutal.

Although he had studied the Bengali language with Thomas on the five-month voyage (during which he was often sick), nothing could have prepared him for the shock of being engulfed in a culture that was not only foreign, but void of any influence of Christianity. One author wrote, "Like Paul at Athens, he was moved by the people's deep-seated religious nature as expressed by the innumerable shrines, the offerings of food and flowers, and the incredible sufferings they readily endured in their quest for spiritual peace. With anguished soul he saw Indian devotees lying on beds of spikes, walking on spiked shoes, swinging themselves on flesh-hooks, gazing at the sun until they lost their sight, and in manifold ways inflicting torture upon their bodies. Most terrible of all was the practice of suttee [sati] or widow-burning. Against this barbaric custom he threw the weight of his utmost energy, until . . . it was finally abolished . . . ."[7]

The Careys' first year in Calcutta was taken up with seeking a place to locate their mission and finding employment. The support from England came slowly and was quickly eaten up by unforeseen expenses. The delay in communication and the lack of responsiveness to needs from the English side (a growing pain of a new organization) meant that unless Carey found employment, their family would starve.

The Lord opened the doors for Carey to become the manager of two indigo factories, a position he held for the following six years. This job not only provided income and a place to live, but it also gave him direct ministry to factory employees. Along with his in-plant duties, his responsibilities included performing inspections throughout the region, and this gave him opportunity to preach as he traveled.

Carey's previous study of language helped him as he tackled the unfamiliar Indian languages. Immediately after settling into the Indigo factory, he began translating the Bible into Bengali. By the time his employment at the factories ended six years later, he had finished the Bengali New Testament.

During those early years, Carey saw no converts, and this of course deeply grieved him. I've had the opportunity to read a collection of his original letters, written in his own beautiful handwriting, to the Baptist Missionary Society in London. These letters are kept today in the Angus Library of Regent's Park College at the University of Oxford, and reading them brings you back to a stifling hot hut in East India where a persistent missionary is reporting to his sending churches. A letter dated December 28, 1796, caught my eye. Its opening sentence reads, "I have purposefully deferred writing to you in hope of having some more pleasing report to communicate than I have as yet sent." Even Carey struggled with writing prayer letters when he did not yet have converts.

But it got worse. The Careys' five-year-old son, Peter, died of dysentery—a blow in itself. Through that experience, Dorothy suffered a nervous breakdown from which she never recovered. Her mind progressively slipped until she died of another illness. Carey wrote again, "Tuesday, December 8, 1807. This evening Mrs. Carey died of the fever under which she has languished some time. Her death was a very easy one; but there was no appearance of returning reason, nor any thing that could cast a dawn of hope or light on her state."

Still Carey soldiered on.

•   •   •   •   •

In 1799, two more missionaries, Joshua Marshman and William Ward, joined Carey in India. The three—Carey, Marshman, and Ward—would labor together for more than two decades, preaching the gospel, planting churches, and translating the Bible into various Indian languages.

The tiny mission group moved to Serampore where Carey accepted a position as the professor of Sanskrit and Bengali languages in Williams College. (The fact that he already was able to lecture not only in a foreign language, but on those languages, speaks to his tenacity of mind in study. He had only been in India for a relatively short time.)

December 28, 1800, was the day for which Carey had longed for seven years. On this day, his first Indian convert, Krishna Pal, made a public profession of salvation as Carey baptized him in the River Ganges. For the next twenty-two years until his death, Pal faithfully served the Lord alongside Carey.

William Carey's Chair: This chair used by William Carey is housed today at St. Andrew's Street Baptist Church in Cambridge, England, which is the church Charles Spurgeon joined after his baptism at age fifteen and the church from where he first began preaching.

Pal's salvation and baptism brought up an issue on which Carey took a strong stand—Hindu castes. The caste system in India was so imbedded into the culture that it would be easy to dismiss it as simply a "cultural difference." But the reality is that it is part of Hinduism and is incompatible with the biblical New Testament church. How can an entire church function as a body if various members refuse to so much as touch one another? How can a church share the Lord's Table when various groups are unable to eat with one another lest they "break caste"?

In his handling of this issue, Carey acted with wisdom and grace. He insisted that new converts break caste, but at the same time, he encouraged every aspect of culture that was purely Indian. He wrote, "We think the great object which Divine Providence has in view in causing the Gospel to be promulgated in the world is not the change of names, the dress, the food, and the innocent usages of mankind, but to produce a moral and divine change in the hearts and conduct of men."[8]

In February of 1801, when Carey completed his translation of the Bengali New Testament, he immediately began translating the Sanskrit New Testament, while at the same time tackling the Bengali Old Testament. The Sanskrit New Testament was published in 1808, and the Bengali Bible completed in 1809. Carey wrote, "I have lived to see the Bible translated into Bengali and the whole New Testament printed."

But Carey's work was far from complete. Even these encouragements were not without hard work and constant setbacks. His wife had just died. He now had the responsibility of teaching a growing number of new converts. He had a constantly-pressing schedule. And always, he pressed forward in the mind-numbing language study and translation.

Years later, Carey wrote, "If, after my removal, anyone should think it worth his while to write my life, I will give you a criterion by which you may judge of its correctness. If he gives me credit for being a plodder, he will describe me justly. Anything beyond this will be too much. *I can plod. I can persevere in any definite pursuit. To this I owe everything.*"

• • • • •

Through William Carey, the plodder, God profoundly blessed India, and these blessings overflowed to the rest of the world.

For the next several years following the completion of the Bengali Bible, Carey worked tirelessly. Carey, Ward, and Marshman (sometimes referred to as "the Serampore trio") had brought in a printing press for the publication of the translated Bibles and tracts. They also hired local help to run the press and took on other printing to help fund their work. (Incidentally, it was Carey, through this printing operation, who introduced printing and paper manufacturing to India.)

On the night of March 11, 1812, a fire raged through the warehouse that held the press, destroying Carey's most recently-translated manuscripts, including a large portion of the Sanskrit Old Testament as well as a polyglot dictionary comparing Sanskrit and its related languages to English and vice versa. The loss was both emotionally and financially staggering. Carey wrote: "In one short evening the labours of years are consumed. How unsearchable are the ways of God! . . . The Lord has laid me low that I may look more simply to Him."[9]

The next morning found Carey back at work retranslating, and six months later, thanks in part to a large offering from Olney Baptist Church as well as other churches, the press was up and running again.

In 1821, the missionaries opened Serampore College primarily to train Christian workers but also offering courses in the arts and sciences. In 1827 Serampore became the first degree-granting institution in Asia.

William Carey's Deathbed: It was on this couch that Carey died in Serampore, India, after forty-one years of gospel ministry in that country.

In 1825, Carey completed the bilingual dictionary of Bengali and English—a literary achievement in its own right and one which became an invaluable help to future missionaries.

In 1829, Carey lived to see the heathen practice of *suttee* abolished. This Hindu custom involved a widow suicidally throwing herself on her husband's burning funeral pyre. From the first time Carey observed a suttee, he did all he could to see it ended. For thirty years, he wrote and spoke out against it. He collected data of instances to combat the excuse that it was never prevalent. (In a single year, he recorded 438 instances within a thirty-mile radius.) Back in England, William Wilberforce used Carey's records and first-hand witness accounts to bring the issue before Parliament. Even before the practice was banned, Wilberforce was successful in using this data and testimony to force a vote requiring the British East India Company to allow missionary activity, significantly increasing the furtherance of the gospel in India. When the edict to abolish suttee came, Carey had the privilege of translating it into Bengali.

• • • • •

Carey suffered his first stroke in the summer of 1833, and his health began to decline quickly. He experienced little pain, but the continuing strokes made him increasingly frail.

Since Dorothy's death, Carey had remarried twice, his second wife Charlotte also having died. His third wife, Grace, now stayed by his side and cared for him.

One of the last people to speak with Carey was Alexander Duff, a young Scottish missionary. After their final conversation, as Duff turned to leave, Carey called him back, "Dr. Duff, you have been speaking about Dr. Carey, Dr. Carey. When I am gone, say nothing about Dr. Carey. Speak about Dr. Carey's Saviour."[10]

As the sun's rays broke over the horizon on June 9, 1834, with his wife and adult children around him, William Carey entered the presence of his Saviour.

Carey had asked to be buried in India, where he had served his Lord for the past forty-one years. At his request, his tombstone has only the dates of his life and a line from a poem by Isaac Watts inscribed:

William Carey
Born August 17, 1761
Died June 9, 1834
"A wretched, poor, and helpless worm, on Thy kind arms I fall."

Carey's legacy is staggering. In his lifetime, he challenged churches worldwide to renew their obedience to the Great Commission. He invested over four decades in preaching the gospel, discipling converts, establishing churches, and training new missionaries—both foreign and national. He confronted heathenism head on and saw the practice of suttee abolished. He personally translated the Bible into multiple languages and oversaw the translating of God's Word into *forty-four* languages and dialects.

One wonders, what if Carey had *not* attempted great things for God? Perhaps more importantly for today, what if *we* don't?

TRUTHS FOR OUTSIDERS

What do we learn from the life of William Carey?

Invest in others. In other words, "Be a John Sutcliff." What was it that Sutcliff saw in Carey that drew him to invest in Carey even when he didn't show obvious pulpit gifts? Sutcliff could have simply told Carey that he should plan to always serve the Lord as a layman. But he didn't; he invested a year of training and future years of support into the man who would become a world changer for missions.

You and I may not be a William Carey, but we can be a John Sutcliff. Who knows whom God will allow us to influence for Him if we are faithful?

Be a personal soulwinner in every sphere of ministry. It is not surprising to me that Carey was a soulwinner in England before he was a missionary to India. From leading his boss to Christ to witnessing to his family to personal soulwinning as a pastor, Carey was concerned for the souls of the people near him—not just the idea of souls in a distant land.

Nothing in the title "pastor" or in the crossing into a foreign country makes a soulwinner. Soulwinning begins from the heart with the compassion of Christ and a genuine care for souls. "Now then we are ambassadors for Christ, as though God did beseech you by us: we pray you in Christ's stead, be ye reconciled to God" (2 Corinthians 5:20).

Gauge your progress by obedient effort, not by evident results. Carey's story is one of perseverance: "I can plod. I can persevere in any definite pursuit. To this I owe everything." Through disappointments and setbacks, discouragement and difficulty, he pressed forward—even without immediate visible results.

But think back to the Moravian missionaries whose testimony so challenged Carey. The Moravians trace back to John Huss who preached and was martyred nearly *four hundred years* before Carey. These early Bohemian and Moravian followers of Christ could have had no idea that their faithful witness would be instrumental in launching the "modern" missions movement nearly four centuries later.

And now think beyond Carey to your own life. Are you seeing less forward progress in your soulwinning or ministry than you would like? Remember that we don't always see the full harvest. Our responsibility is obedient faithfulness. "And let us not be weary in well doing: for in due season we shall reap, if we faint not" (Galatians 6:9).

Encourage missionaries in patient perseverance. Foreign missionaries often face unique challenges in sharing the gospel and planting churches. Like Carey in India, often they are ministering in a culture that is completely ignorant of spiritual truth. It takes time and persistent effort. Be careful not to pressure missionaries to report results, but encourage them in continued persistence and faithful planting of the gospel seed.

Expect great things from God; attempt great things for God. Do you believe that God still wants to work mightily in the world today? Would you be willing to give your all to attempt something great for Him?

GEORGE MÜLLER
(1805–1898)

"Faith does not operate in the realm of the possible. There is no glory for God in that which is humanly possible. Faith begins where man's power ends."

George Müller

D o you believe God is real?

Do you believe He answers prayer?

These sound like rhetorical, perhaps ridiculous, questions. But considering how great our needs and the needs surrounding us are, I'm not sure our actual prayer lives answer these questions in the affirmative.

In the life and legacy of George Müller, however, we find a man whose heartbeat was to answer these questions, not just for himself, but for the benefit of Christians around the world. His faith-filled prayer life challenges me, and anyone who takes time to study Müller's life will see a clearer picture of what the Lord can do in their own life.

In his lifetime, Müller cared for over ten thousand orphans, with no salary, no fundraising, no borrowing, and no making his needs known to others. Perhaps even more significantly, one of his chief aims was realized, as he proved to the world that God is real and is ready and able to meet our needs and enable us to minister for Him in extraordinary ways.

• • • • •

There are those who seem destined for greatness from their earliest years. Whether because of royal birth, academic prowess, or an inner drive to succeed, some individuals are marked even as children or teenagers as those who are very likely to succeed. George Müller was not among them. His youthful days were marked by dishonesty, filled with shiftless living, and scarred by immorality.

Müller was born in Prussia on September 27, 1805, into a well-to-do family. At the age of ten, he attended a classical school at Halberstadt, intended to prepare him for university. One night when George was fourteen, his mother died while he was out at a tavern playing cards with his friends. He spent much of the next day drinking, unaware of his mother's death. Müller's father decided to bring George back home to live with him, where George could study under a tutor.

But Müller wasn't particularly studious. By the time he was a teenager, he was far more skilled in stealing money from his friends and tax-collector father than he was in any particular field of study. Müller used this money to fund a playboy lifestyle, which he kept hidden from his father.

Raised in the Lutheran church, Müller attended confirmation classes the same year his mother died. On the eve of his confirmation, he was expected to make a formal confession of his sin, paying the clergyman as he did so. He used the opportunity to cheat the clergyman out of eleven-twelfths of the fee his father had given him.

When Müller was sixteen years old, his appetite for extravagant and licentious living caught up with him when he didn't quite make it out of his hotel before it became evident he couldn't pay his bill. He spent several weeks in prison until his father reluctantly bailed him out by paying the bill.

Müller's father was desperate to make his son into a reputable member of society who would bring his father respect and whose earnings would be sufficient to care for his father in old age. With these motives, he sent Müller to the University of Halle in 1824 to study for the ministry.

As a nineteen-year-old university student, Müller made a genuine effort to turn over a new leaf, largely to gain his father's approval. His sinful ways, however, followed him to Halle, and the lying, stealing, drinking, and immoral living proved impossible to shake.

One of Müller's friends invited Müller to a Christian Bible study, and he decided to attend. For the first time, Müller saw New Testament Christianity—not the forms of religion he had grown up with, but true believers in Christ studying His Word and filled with His love, joy, and peace.

Müller couldn't get enough of it. He went again and again.

Although Müller was studying for the ministry, he had no Bible and had not read one in years. He later explained that he had never so much as heard of the new birth: "I had never met with a person who told me that he meant to live, by the help of God, according to the Scriptures. In short, I had not the least idea that there were any persons really different from myself, except in degree."[1]

In time, Müller came to understand the glorious gospel of Christ and was born again. His life dramatically transformed—both inside and out. Not only did Müller put away the sins for which he was so well known around the university campus, but his entire focus and direction in life changed. He wanted to be a missionary.

While it would seem that Müller's father would be thrilled for the changes in George's life, the opposite was true. He became angry at the prospect of losing the respect and income that would have been his had George settled into a career in the highly esteemed German Lutheran church.

George wrote of this turn of events:

My father was greatly displeased, and particularly reproached me, that he had expended so much money on my education, in hope that he might comfortably spend his last days with me in a parsonage, and that he now saw all these prospects come to nothing. He was angry, and told me he would no longer consider me as his son. But the Lord gave me grace to remain steadfast. He then entreated me, and wept before me, yet even this far harder trial the Lord enabled me to bear. . . . After I had left my father I determined, though I wanted [stood in need of] more money than at any previous period of my life, as I had to remain two years longer in the university, never to take any more money from him; for it seemed to me wrong, so far as I remember, to suffer myself to be supported by him, when he had no prospect that I should become what he would wish me to be, namely, a clergyman with a good living. This I have been enabled to act out.[2]

God provided for Müller, and he worked his way through the final two years of university tutoring American students in German and translating German lectures for English-speaking students.

One of the special provisions of God took place in the form of lodging at Francke's Orphan House, provided free of charge to poor divinity students. This orphanage was started by Hermann Francke, a born-again professor of theology at Halle, who, moved by the needs of street children, opened a home for them, depending solely on God for provision. Thus, in God's divine providence, Müller's financial needs brought him face to face with a pattern of what would comprise much of his future life work.

• • • • •

After graduation in 1829, a position opened for Müller to become a missionary to the Jews in London. Shortly after arriving in the city, he became ill and traveled to Exeter by the coast for rest. While there, he met two people whom God would use throughout his life.

The first was Henry Craik, a Scottish preacher, about the same age as George, who would become a lifelong friend and co-laborer in gospel ministry. The following January, Craik invited Müller to move to Exeter and pastor the Baptist church in nearby Teignmouth, which he did.

After moving to Exeter, Müller met the second person who would be God's gift to him for the next forty years—Mary Groves, a godly young woman with similar convictions as George and a shared desire to serve the Lord wherever and how ever He should lead them. George proposed in August, and they married on October 7, 1830.

It was during this period of Müller's life that he and Mary began developing and living out the convictions regarding prayer and faith which they would follow in the years to come. Specifically, they gave away all of their savings and valuables to the poor and determined that they would not make their needs known to others but would trust the Lord alone to provide for them as they sought Him in prayer. At the same time, they lived generously, giving away much of Müller's small salary. They found that God was faithful.

In 1832, Craik invited Müller to join him in Bristol, a port city eighty miles northeast, to help in the new pastorate Craik had just accepted. Together, Müller and Craik pastored two churches—the Gideon Chapel and the Bethesda Chapel. Müller would continue to pastor the Bethesda Chapel until his death. In early 1834, they founded the Scriptural Knowledge Institution, established to aid Sunday schools, circulate Scripture, and help missionaries. Through this endeavor, Müller continued to practice his faith-living principles with a commitment to never go into debt and never take out a loan.

But the great platform for proving God's faithfulness and power to hear and answer prayer was yet ahead.

• • • • •

Indian cholera broke out in England in 1831, and by the following summer, it was an epidemic in Bristol. By the time Müller arrived there, cholera had claimed the lives of many, leaving hundreds of children orphaned and destitute. The children would either go live with relatives, many of whom struggled to make ends meet to feed their own children, or they would be sent to the workhouses where they would be forced to work harder than grown adults are today, sometimes to the children's deaths. The third option was to live as street children.

Müller couldn't help but be touched by the plight of the street children in Bristol. Treated almost as vermin by respectable citizens, the street children had no choice but to beg for food. Out of necessity, many resorted to stealing.

Charles Dickens wrote about the wretched condition of orphaned children in his serial novel (1837–1839), *Oliver Twist,* by which he sought to awaken the conscience of a nation. But Müller didn't need a story to see the need in front of him and to care. He had the Word of God which told him, "Pure religion and undefiled before God and the Father is this, To visit the fatherless and widows in their affliction, and to keep himself unspotted from the world" (James 1:27).

In 1836, Müller brought the needs of the orphaned children before his church family with a definite plan to open his own home for orphan girls. He invited his church family to pray with them that God would supply the staff, supplies, and funds. The church gave and volunteered generously, and soon, the £1,000 for which Müller was praying was in hand.

On April 21, 1836, the new home, which could house thirty girls, received their first orphans at 6 Wilson Street in Bristol and was soon filled to capacity.

God continued to provide financially, and in October of the same year, the Müllers rented 1 Wilson Street and opened it for orphan infants, both boys and girls. This home, too, was soon filled to capacity.

Just seven months later, the Müllers again stepped out in faith and rented a third house at 3 Wilson Street—this time for boys.

By 1845, the Müllers were renting four houses on Wilson Street, housing a total of 130 children. That fall, the inevitable happened: neighbors complained that the noise from the overcrowded homes was disturbing the peace.

To turn away children already taken in wasn't an option. And the applications from more needy children continued pouring in. What could be done?

* * * * *

What is sometimes missed in the telling of Müller's incredible story is that his motive in opening the orphan houses was more than compassion for the orphans. In fact, compassion was his second motivation.

To fully understand Müller's primary motive, it's important to remember the time period in which this story unfolded. German rationalism, which denied the divinity of Christ as well as miracles of the Bible and additionally questioned even the existence of God, was sweeping Europe, leaving skepticism and atheism in its wake. Many professing Christians began embracing liberal theology, and others were shaken in their faith. And still others, perhaps the majority, simply lived as if God were only for Sundays. They attended church but had no vibrancy in their relationship with the Lord and no expectation that He would answer their prayers.

Müller, then, wanted to prove to others what he had already been experiencing—that God *is* real, that He *does* answer prayer, and that He personally and powerfully cares for His own.

Before Müller even presented the needs of the orphans to his church, God had directed his attention to Psalm 81:10, "I am the Lord thy God, which brought thee out of the land of Egypt: open thy mouth wide, and I will fill it." This promise became a rock to which he returned repeatedly as he prayed for God's provision in meeting the needs of the orphans in his care.

The stories of God's direct provision are numerous. Funds were often tight, frequently nonexistent. But the children never went hungry, the rent never went unpaid, and the homes were never left unable to provide clothing, food, or education on a day-to-day basis.

Perhaps the most famous incident of God's provision in answer to prayer took place on the morning Müller was told that they had no money and no food to give the children for the next day's breakfast. Müller prayed most of the night.

The following morning, a Christian baker in the city came by with freshly-baked bread—enough for all four houses of orphans. He related that as he went to bed the evening before, God had specifically impressed on him that he should get up and make bread for Müller's orphans.

Müller's Desk: It was a special experience when in Bristol a few years ago to sit at Müller's desk where he recorded the many instances of God's miraculous provision in answer to prayer.

No sooner had the baker left the orphanage than the local milkman knocked on the door. The wheel on his horse-drawn milk cart had broken off just outside the orphan houses. He wondered if the orphans could use the milk he had to unload in order to fix the cart.

Müller kept meticulous records of their funds, donors, and needs. His autobiography records many such miraculous answers to prayer.

George and Mary Müller gave liberally of their own funds. In fact, they made it their practice to continually empty their accounts and sell any accumulated valuables for the orphans or to send to missionaries around the world anytime a need in the orphan houses arose. This gave them greater liberty as they prayed for God to supernaturally meet the needs of the orphans.

The faith and prayer with which Müller lived can be summed up in his journal entry from November 12, 1839, "But I am not looking at the little in hand, but at the fullness of God."[3]

• • • • •

The limited occupancy and the neighbors' complaints were not Müller's only concerns for the four overcrowded children's homes on Wilson Street. He also believed the children needed outdoor space to play and to work. In 1845, he began definitely praying for a new location to which to move the homes.

In 1846, the Lord provided for Müller to purchase a beautiful piece of property in Ashley Down, just outside the city limits. The owner of the property gave Müller a steep discount, and a Christian architect volunteered his services for free. Having purposed to never take a loan or go into debt, and to never begin a building project without the full funds in hand prior to breaking ground, Müller prayed, planned, and waited. By 1847, God had provided all of the funds to complete the first home, and building began.

In 1849, the first house at Ashley Down was complete. It had accommodations for three hundred children, and it was quickly filled to capacity.

In 1851, with seventy-eight children on a waiting list for the orphanage, Müller determined to build a second home on the same property. It was completed debt free in 1857, and immediately after its completion, construction began on a third home.

By 1870, there were a total of five large orphan dormitories at Ashley Down, with the ability to house up to 2,050 children at one time.

Müller, just like anyone who sets out to do a great work for God, was not without his critics. Charles Dickens, hearing rumors that the children were ill-kept and starving, traveled from London to Bristol to drop in unannounced and see for himself. What he found so encouraged him that he wrote an article titled "Brother Müller and His Orphan Work," which was published in the newspaper on November 7, 1857.

Several years ago, Terrie and I had the opportunity to visit Ashley Down, and although the work continues today, it is on more of a foster family basis throughout the city. As we viewed the original buildings which are now used for classrooms and residential housing, we were amazed at Müller's vision, not only for the physical needs of the orphans, but for their academic and spiritual needs as well. All of Müller's orphans were given a good education with an emphasis placed on learning trades that would prepare them to support themselves as adults. (Some people even complained that Müller was providing *such* a good education that he was raising the poor out of their natural station—a fear among some in Victorian Britain.) Most importantly, many of the orphans trusted Christ as their Saviour.

• • • • •

On February 6, 1870, Mary Müller went to be with the Lord. Her husband's sense of loss was profound, but he continued in the work. About the same time, James Wright, who would soon marry the Müller's only daughter, Lydia, was appointed as Müller's assistant and successor to the orphanage work.

The following year, Müller married Susannah Sanger, a godly woman who had served as a matron in the orphanages. In the coming years, Susannah encouraged Müller to accept the international speaking engagements he had declined previously in order to continue his work. Pointing out that he now had capable people to oversee the orphanage and a unique testimony of God's faithfulness, Susannah was successful

God Answers Prayer: This quote by Müller references what is probably the greatest legacy of his life—proving the willingness of God to answer prayer.

in encouraging George to leave the orphanages with James and Lydia Wright and share with others around the world the story of God's goodness with others.

Even in these journeys, Müller continued to see God's willingness to answer prayer. Once while crossing the Atlantic Ocean, the ship became engulfed in a dense fog bank and had to stop. Müller made his way to the wheelhouse and informed the captain, "I have come to tell you that I must be in Quebec on Saturday afternoon. I have never broken an engagement in fifty years." The captain replied that he could do nothing in light of the bad weather.

"Let us go down to the chart room and pray," Müller said. As the captain told the story a few weeks later to Evangelist Charles Inglis, he said, "I looked at the man of God, and I thought to myself, what lunatic asylum could the man have come from? I never heard of such a thing." He asked Müller, "Do you know how dense the fog is?"

"No," Müller replied. "My eye is not on the density of the fog, but on the living God who controls every circumstance of my life." Müller prayed for the fog to lift in five minutes. The captain asked if he should pray, but Müller said, "I believe God has answered. There is no need to pray." Within moments the fog was gone, and they were on their way.[4]

Over the next seventeen years, the Müllers traveled together as he preached in forty-two countries, including the United States four times and India twice.

In 1890, Müller's daughter Lydia died, and in 1894, Susannah died. Alone and eighty-eight years old, Müller's testimony never dampened but continued to be one of joy in the Lord, faithfulness in prayer, and regularly-answered prayer.

In fact, Müller's final answer to prayer occurred after his death. For more than fifty years he had prayed specifically for five of his friends from his university days. Four were saved over the years (one of these shortly before his death), and the final friend was saved a few months after Müller's passing into Heaven.

Müller wrote, "The great fault of the children of God is, they do not continue in prayer; they do not go on praying; they do not persevere. If they desire anything for God's glory, they should pray until they get it."[5]

• • • • •

On March 10, 1898, ninety-two year old Müller rose to spend time with the Lord as he did every morning before handling the orphanage's correspondence and preparing his message for Sunday. A few hours later, he was found collapsed in his study, already in the presence of the Lord.

The entire city of Bristol came to a standstill for Müller's funeral as thousands lined the streets to pay their last respects. His life had made a dramatic impact on his city.

The Daily Telegraph wrote of Müller that he ". . . had robbed the cruel streets of thousands of victims, the gaols [jails] of thousands of felons, the workhouses of thousands of helpless waifs."[6]

The Bristol Times touched on Müller's own passion when it reported, "He was raised up for the purpose of showing that the age of miracles is not past, and rebuking the sceptical tendencies of the time."[7]

During his lifetime, Müller had stewarded over $7 million in donations (worth over $250 million today). He had overseen the care and education of over ten thousand orphans. And he had proved to the world that God answers prayer.

TRUTHS FOR OUTSIDERS

What do we learn from the life of George Müller?

Never underestimate the value of sharing the gospel with one person. Though Müller wasn't saved as a child, and as a young adult he didn't seem to have an interest in spiritual things, God was still working in his heart. God wonderfully used the pure-hearted faith of Christians in a Bible study to convict Müller of his need for Christ.

As believers, may we never write off someone as a candidate for God's grace and the powerful transformation of the gospel.

Show the love of Christ to those others neglect. In this day of armchair critics and political virtue signalers, it is refreshing to see someone who personally and tangibly loved the needy and who served those who could never repay him, sharing with them the love of Christ and influencing them for eternity.

God delights in answering persevering prayer. Müller wasn't a super saint who had special access to God that you and I do not have. He was a faithful Christian who took advantage of God's invitation to prayer and proved that God means what He says and keeps His promises. Müller wrote, "I live in the spirit of prayer. I pray as I walk, when I lie down, and when I rise. And the answers are always coming. Tens of thousands of times my prayers have been answered. When once I am persuaded a thing is right, I go on praying for it until the end comes. I never give up!"[8] At another time he said, "The great fault of the children of God is, they do not continue in prayer; they do not go on praying; they do not persevere. If they desire anything for God's glory, they should pray until they get it. Oh, how good, and kind, and gracious, and condescending is the One with Whom we have to do! He has given me, unworthy as I am, immeasurably above all I had asked or thought!"[9]

That same God wants you to take advantage of His same invitation, and He wants to show you in the same way He showed George Müller that He is still the same prayer-answering God.

God blesses a life of prayer and faith. Perhaps the single greatest truth we learn from Müller's life is that God still calls us to "walk by faith, not by sight" (2 Corinthians 5:7), and He still blesses the life lived in simple dependence upon Him.

When we feel overwhelmed with the needs surrounding us, when we feel inadequate for the responsibilities and callings before us, may we look to Christ, live on our knees, and rejoice in His faithfulness.

12

HORATIUS BONAR

(1808–1889)

"Whatever the way be—rough, gloomy, unpleasant—we press forward, knowing that the same grace that has already carried thousands through will do the same for us."

Horatius Bonar

Among the 100,000 volumes in our West Coast Baptist College library, there are over a dozen books written by Horatius Bonar. These include titles such as *Words to Winners of Souls, God's Way of Holiness, The Night of Weeping, Christ the Healer, Historical Collections of Accounts of Revival,* and several commentaries.

But among all of these volumes, there is not a single full-length book written about Bonar. This is because he requested no memoir be written of his life.

Yet, for as little-known as Bonar is, God used him in significant ways. Even as the sample book titles above suggest, Bonar was a soulwinner, pastor, and committed Christian who greatly influenced a nation. Most significantly, he was Scotland's greatest hymn writer.

Since there were no memoirs published of his life, I present simply an introduction to this man worthy of our study.

●　●　●　●　●

Horatius Bonar, called Horace by his friends, was born on December 9, 1808 in Edinburgh, Scotland to James and Marjory Bonar. Of Bonar's parents' eleven children, at least three of their sons became preachers—John, Horace, and Andrew.

Horatius wasn't the only writer in the family, as his younger brother, Andrew, is also remembered as an author. Among other books, Andrew wrote the biography of Robert Murray M'Cheyne (who was a friend of both Horace and Andrew). Andrew's own journals are published as well.

As a boy, Bonar was surrounded by godly influences. Although his father, who died when Horace was twelve years old, was a lawyer, the family was part of a long line of preachers; and Horace was greatly impacted by his godly mother.

Godly influences continued throughout Bonar's life. One of his professors at the University of Edinburgh was Dr. Thomas Chalmers, who loved the Lord and greatly influenced Bonar in his walk with Christ. The godly Robert Murray M'Cheyne, whose biography Andrew Bonar wrote, was one of Horace's classmates and a close friend.

We don't know at what point Bonar trusted Christ as his Saviour, but that he did is sure. Bonar strongly believed and clearly preached in the necessity of the new birth and a personal choice to trust Christ as Saviour.

> If Christ be not the *Substitute*, he is nothing to the sinner. If he did not die as the Sinbearer, he has died in vain. Let us not be deceived on this point, nor misled by those who, when they announce Christ as the Deliverer, think they have preached the gospel. If I throw a rope to a drowning man, I am a deliverer. But is Christ no more than that? If I cast myself into the sea and *risk* myself to save another, I am a deliverer. But is Christ no

more? Did he but *risk* His life? The very essence of Christ's deliverance is the substitution of himself for us, his life for ours. He did not come to *risk* his life; he came to die! He did not redeem us by a little loss, a little sacrifice, a little labor, a little suffering: "He redeemed us to God by His blood," (Revelation 5:9); "the precious blood of Christ," (1 Peter 1:19). He gave all he had, even his life, for us. This is the kind of deliverance that awakens the happy song, "Unto him that loved us, and washed us from our sins in his own blood" (Revelation 1:5).[1]

Bonar was ordained to the gospel ministry in 1837 and began pastoring the Church of Scotland at Kelso.

• • • • •

In 1843, Bonar married Jane Catherine Lundie, and they shared the next forty years together. Although the Lord blessed the Bonars with several children, five died at young ages. Bonar always maintained a tenderness in his heart toward children. In fact, it was for children whom Bonar first began composing hymns.

Bonar's introduction into hymn writing parallels Isaac Watts' experience. You may remember hearing that Watts (1674–1748), as a teenager, complained to his father of the dry hymns and lack-luster singing in church. His father challenged him to write better songs. He began that week with the hymn "Behold the Glories of the Lamb" and introduced it the following Sunday to the nonconformist church he attended. It was received with enthusiasm, and Watts continued writing a hymn nearly every week for the next two years. He later published these in *Hymns and Spiritual Songs*. This collection contained "When I Survey the Wondrous Cross," "O God, Our Help in Ages Past," "I Sing the Mighty Power of God," "Am I a Soldier of the Cross?" and "Joy to the World."

Bonar's start to hymn writing had a similar motive to Watts', but his purpose was reversed. As a Scottish pastor, he noticed the psalter singing of the church (comprised of paraphrased Psalms set to poetic meter) wasn't captivating the children in his congregation. Thus, he began writing fresh songs for them.

Entitled "The Substitute," his first hymn is often referred to today by its first line, "I lay my sins on Jesus."

> I lay my sins on Jesus,
> The spotless Lamb of God;
> He bears them all, and frees us
> From the accursed load:
>
> I bring my guilt to Jesus,
> To wash my crimson stains
> White in His blood most precious,
> 'Til not a spot remains.

The biography that Bonar shunned is at least in part written through his hymns. We see through them his doctrine, his trust, and his heart. Perhaps his most well-known hymn is "I Heard the Voice of Jesus Say."

> I heard the voice of Jesus say,
> Come unto Me and rest;
> Lay down, thou weary one, lay down
> Thy head upon My breast!"
> I came to Jesus as I was,
> Weary, and worn, and sad;
> I found in Him a resting-place,
> And He hath made me glad.
>
> I heard the voice of Jesus say,
> Behold, I freely give
> The living water; thirsty one,
> Stoop down, and drink, and live!"
> I came to Jesus, and I drank
> Of that life-giving stream;
> My thirst was quenched, my soul revived,
> And now I live in Him.

I heard the voice of Jesus say,
I am this dark world's Light;
Look unto Me, thy morn shall rise,
And all thy day be bright!"
I looked to Jesus, and I found
In Him my Star, my Sun;
And in that Light of life I'll walk
Till trav'ling days are done.

Another of his hymns which speaks of his great trust in the Lord's paths and may be familiar to many is "Thy Way, Not Mine, O Lord."

Thy way, not mine, O Lord,
However dark it be!
Lead me by Thine own hand,
Choose out the path for me.

Smooth let it be or rough,
It will be still the best;
Winding or straight, it leads
Right onward to Thy rest.

Throughout Bonar's ministry, he eventually wrote over six hundred hymns. Today, he is known as "The Prince of Scottish Hymn Writers."

Bonar's hymns are not as familiar to me as Watts' or some of the other English hymn writers', but every time I read their lyrics, which are full of joy and trust and anticipation for Christ's return, I'm blessed. As Isaac Watts and Charles Wesley became England's hymnodists and Fanny Crosby became the United States', Bonar became Scotland's.

• • • • •

The year 1843 brought a significant change in Bonar's ministry. In that year, the Church of Scotland went through a split in which the evangelical leaders left the Established Church to form the Free Church of Scotland.

Four hundred fifty pastors walked out of the General Assembly Meeting, and the event became known as "The Disruption of 1843."

The reasons for this split related to the mixing of church and state which always becomes problematic in a state church. (This is one of the reasons I believe so strongly in the autonomy of the local church, as modeled in the New Testament.) The most pressing issue had to do with the government appointing pastors to each parish church, rather than congregations calling their own pastors, or at least having veto power to deny a candidate they believed was unfit for the office. As you might guess, government appointments became politically influenced, and as a result, churches were finding themselves obligated to pastors who were liberal in theology and unfit for the office personally.

Thomas Chalmers, Bonar's theology professor from his university days, was among those who led in forming the Free Church. It was a courageous decision. All of the pastors who left the Church of Scotland also left behind their financial support, parsonage homes, and, of course, their congregations.

The Free Church now had to build from scratch without any financing from the state. This included church buildings across Scotland as well as a school in which to train their pastors for the ministry. The group founded New College, within the University of Edinburgh, and appointed Thomas Chalmers as its first principal. It opened its doors in November of 1843 to almost two hundred students.

Bonar joined in this movement, fully supporting it from the outset. Years later, in 1883, Bonar served as the Moderator of the General Assembly for the Free Church of Scotland.

Throughout Bonar's fifty-year ministry, he was known for many of his godly and ministry-hearted attributes. But he was also known for a specific doctrine to which he held—the premillennial return of Christ. Contrary to the prevalent teaching at the University of Edinburgh, Bonar believed that Jesus will one day reign on Earth for a literal one thousand years (the Millennium) and that He will bodily return before that time (premillennial return). He based these convictions (as I do) on Isaiah 11:4–8, Matthew 24:30, Acts 1:11, Revelation 1:7, 1 Thessalonians 5:2, and many other passages.

In 1856, Bonar was among four men (two of the others being his brother Andrew and Robert Murray M'Cheyne) commissioned by the Free Church of Scotland to visit Jews in Palestine. A guest from another group happened upon a service which Bonar was leading and related the following story. It is particularly interesting to me for its description of Bonar himself as well as the significance of his premillennial beliefs in this setting.

One dark night in the year 1856, in the city Jerusalem, I wandered into a lighted mission-room on Mount Zion, where a small company of men and women of various nationalities and complexions were gathered. At the desk was a man of impressive countenance, of low and musical voice . . . .

The preacher, as I learned later, was Dr. Horatius Bonar. Learned and eloquent, there was a wonderful charm in what he said that night, because he had strong convictions on that subject of much speculation— the second coming of the Lord. He believed in His personal coming, to reign on the earth; and his faith, seconded by his rich poetic imagination and fervor, all quickened by the fact that we were in Jerusalem, the city of the Passion, the Crucifixion, the Resurrection and the Ascension gave to his words a winning power which I cannot describe. He had no specific time for the Advent. He did not argue in controversy, but gave himself up to the scene where, sooner or later, the King shall come again to walk in the streets of His abasement, in the effulgence of the sunlight that shall attend Him. . . . To hear such a man in Jerusalem, having a firm belief in the personal coming and reign of Christ, thus to communicate to others freely his confident hopes, was a memorable event.[2]

Bonar's adherence to the premillennial return of Christ is one of the reasons I especially enjoy his hymns. Sound doctrine makes for good singing! And this doctrine in particular is one which God has revealed to us specifically to bring comfort to our hearts (1 Thessalonians 4:16–18).

●　●　●　●　●

Because of Bonar's request that no biography be written of him, almost the only place to learn information about him is in chapter-length sketches in books about hymn writers. These sketches culminate in a picture of a well-rounded Christian leader whose dedication to Christ shone through in every area of his life.

As a pastor, Bonar was as committed as any shepherd ever was. One author wrote, "He was always visiting, always preaching, always writing and always praying."[3] In 1867, he moved from his church in Kelso to Edinburgh to begin pastoring the Chalmers Memorial Church, named in honor of his previous teacher.

As a Christian, Bonar gave great attention to his walk with God and living a life of holiness. He was regular and fervent in the spiritual disciplines of Bible study and prayer, so much so that a servant girl in the Bonar house came to see her need for Christ by watching his example. Seeing his frequent times in private prayer, she said to herself, "If he needs to pray so much, what will become of me if I do not pray?"[4] This spark of conviction eventually led to her trusting Christ as her Saviour.

As a soulwinner, Bonar was consistent. He wrote and published gospel tracts, and he constantly looked for opportunities to point a lost soul to faith in Christ. Once while counseling a young man who felt his sin was too great for God to forgive, Bonar asked him, "Tell me, which is of greater weight in the eyes of God—your sin, black as it is, or the blood of Jesus shed for sinners?" A light came into the

Church Pews: Kirk of the Canongate: Bonar is buried behind this kirk (church). Ever since Queen Elizabeth II visited the church on her first visit to Edinburgh as a reigning sovereign in 1952, the royal family worships here when in Edinburgh.

young man's eyes as he recognized the significance of Christ's sacrifice for his sin. He trusted Christ on the spot.[5]

As a husband, father, and grandfather, Bonar was faithful and caring. As mentioned previously, he and his wife Jane were married for forty years. Later in their lives, one of their surviving daughters was widowed and, with her five children, came to live with her parents. While some couples who are up in years might struggle with caring for little ones again, Bonar was filled with joy at the opportunity and saw it as the Lord's way of giving him five more children after the five he and Jane had lost.

One of the most stirring quotes from all Bonar's writings is from his sermon "The Desert Pillar."

The road is rugged, and the sun is hot. How can we be but weary? Here is grace for the weariness—grace which lifts us up and invigorates us; grace which keeps us from fainting by the way; grace which supplies us with manna from heaven, and with water from the smitten rock. We receive of this grace, and are revived. Our weariness of heart and limb departs. We need no other refreshment. This is enough. Whatever the way be—rough, gloomy, unpleasant—we press forward, knowing that the same grace that has already carried thousands through will do the same for us.[6]

Bonar's desire was to point people not to himself, but to Christ. This was his motive in requesting, as he neared the end of his earthly journey, that no biography be written about him. He didn't want misplaced credit for what God had done through him.

Bonar died on July 31, 1889. He was buried at Canongate Kirkyard in Edinburgh. His hymns and writings continue to point us to Christ, and Bonar's lifelong wish is fulfilled.

TRUTHS FOR OUTSIDERS

What do we learn from the life of Horatius Bonar?

Well-known does not necessarily equal greatly-used. If there is a caution to be given in studying the lives of men and women greatly used by God, it is that we not subconsciously come to believe that greatness for God will equate with recognition by others or a legacy of biographies to be written of us. The fact that Bonar's name is little-recognized by Christians today doesn't mean he was less fruitful than, say, John Knox who is well-known. In fact, for the members of Bonar's congregation, how well-remembered his name might be two centuries later had zero impact on his ministry to them. For the Christians around the world who have been blessed by Bonar's hymns, the fact that they know little if anything of the author doesn't lessen the comfort or strength they receive from the hymns.

To every man or woman laboring for Christ in unseen, unknown, unrecognized places, remember that lack of recognition doesn't mean your efforts are less impactful for Christ. God sees, and He blesses. "For God is not unrighteous to forget your work and labour of love, which ye have shewed toward his name, in that ye have ministered to the saints, and do minister" (Hebrews 6:10).

Our theology affects our outlook. If there is another misconception which Bonar's life clears up, it is that theology only matters in seminary halls or a pastor's study. The reality is that what we believe about God and learn from His Word impacts every other area of our lives. In Bonar's case, his biblical view of eschatology (the end times) birthed hymns full of hope regarding Christ's return.

Second Timothy 2:15 admonishes us, "Study to shew thyself approved unto God, a workman that needeth not to be ashamed, rightly dividing the word of truth." As we study God's Word, it gives us a heavenly perspective.

Spiritual disciplines impact the greater picture of our fruitfulness. We cannot expect fruitful work for God without spending regular time with God. Soulwinning, preaching, and other visible aspects of ministry will only sustain long-term fruitfulness as they are rooted in a growing relationship with the Lord and personal time with Him. Public ministry must be built on the private spiritual disciplines of Bible reading and study and prayer.

Jesus told His disciples in John 15:4, "Abide in me, and I in you. As the branch cannot bear fruit of itself, except it abide in the vine; no more can ye, except ye abide in me." If you want to be fruitful for God, spend time with God.

DAVID LIVINGSTONE
(1813–1873)

"Anywhere, provided it be forward."

David Livingstone

Scotland saw him as a great explorer. The history books deem him a geographer. Social activists consider him an abolitionist. He reckoned himself a missionary. He was David Livingstone, and he opened the continent of Africa to the gospel.

The feats David Livingstone accomplished are remarkable. He was the first European to view the breathtaking Victoria Falls in Zambia. He filled in large sections of the otherwise empty maps of Africa, tracing the Zambezi and Congo throughout the continent. He was the first European to cross the southern portion of Africa from coast to coast.

And he did all of this on sheer willpower. That is to say, Livingstone didn't have skills, abilities, or opportunities not available to any ordinary person. He became a medical doctor, and he taught himself the geographic skills necessary to forge his way ahead and map where he had been. But that alone is not what pushed him through the fever-infested jungles of Africa with warring tribes in constant need.

So what *did* drive Livingstone? What compelled him forward when every other reasonable man would quit . . . or not even begin?

It wasn't the accolades. It wasn't the book sales. It wasn't the gold medals from the Royal Geographic Society. Although Livingstone received all of these, they could not have compelled him to bury his life in Africa. He had a higher motive.

Livingstone's sense of calling traces back to a meeting he attended as a twenty-seven-year-old medical missionary candidate. There he heard pioneer missionary to Africa, Robert Moffat, tell his audience, "I have sometimes seen, in the morning sun, the smoke of a thousand villages—villages whose people are without Christ, without God, and without hope in the world."

Something inside of Livingstone reached toward those villages. He must go to them.

• • • • •

Nearly two hundred years before Livingstone's birth, the soil of Scotland was tilled by her martyrs who gave their lives for the sake of the gospel. Patrick Hamilton, George Wishart, and others could not have guessed how God would bring revival fruit through their lives nearly two centuries later. And David Livingstone was part of that fruit.

On March 19, 1813, David Livingstone was born to poor but godly Christian parents in Blantyre, Scotland. The whole family lived in a one-room tenement apartment with their seven children.

When he was ten years old, Livingstone began working in a cotton mill to help support the family. All day long, from 6:00 a.m. to 8:00 p.m., he walked back and forth under the looms, his body bent over double, piecing together cotton threads that became separated, so the finished cloth would be flawless. After fourteen hours at the mill, Livingstone attended night school for two more hours. Hungry to learn more, he bought himself a basic Latin grammar, and when he was promoted to the job of spinning at the mill, he propped his book up at eye level on the loom so he could study while he worked. Already, his indomitable perseverance was developing.

Livingstone Memorial: This statue of Livingstone stands in Edinburgh as a tribute to one of Scotland's finest men.

Even as a knowledge-hungry child, Livingstone was suited for action. He loved reading both travel and scientific discovery books.

As a teenager, Livingstone came to understand the simple gospel and placed his faith in Christ. He said that in that moment, he felt like a person cured of color-blindness.[1] Old things were passed away, and all things were made new (2 Corinthians 5:17). "It is my desire," he wrote, "to show my attachment to the cause of Him who died for me, by devoting my life to his service." Thirty-nine years later, from the heart of Africa, Livingstone reiterated this desire on what would be his second-to-last birthday: "My birthday! My Jesus, my King, my Life, my All. I again this time dedicate my whole self to Thee."[2]

Livingstone's reading brought him into contact with Henry Martyn (1781–1812), missionary to India and Persia, as well as Charles Gutzlaff

(1803–1851), a medical missionary to China. The testimony of these two men profoundly impacted Livingstone, and he determined to serve the Lord as a medical missionary. He put himself through college and medical school and applied to the London Missionary Society to serve in China.

Just after Livingstone's acceptance by the London Missionary Society in 1838, the Opium War broke out in China (1839–1842). The society decided it would not be best to send a new missionary to such a volatile situation. But the war dragged on, and Livingstone became weary of waiting.

It was at this juncture, in 1840, that Livingstone heard Missionary Robert Moffat share the needs of Africa. While many people would feel fearful of a foreign land with as much still unknown as Africa was to the average European at the time, Livingstone was captivated. He listened carefully as Moffat shared the spiritual needs, heathen customs, and dearth of missionaries. Livingstone was drawn by the reality that there were millions of people who had never heard the gospel and yet lived beyond where any foreign missionary had been.

In the following weeks, Livingstone requested that the London Missionary Society send him to Africa rather than China. He received permission, packed his medicines and supplies, and set sail for Cape Town, South Africa. Although Livingstone's steps had been redirected, he had no doubt that he was being led by the hand of God.

• • • • •

Livingstone's first decade in Africa was spent primarily in preaching and establishing mission stations. From Cape Town, he went 650 miles inland to Kuruman, where Robert Moffat and his wife Mary had been serving since 1820 (and would continue until 1870). Here he assisted

Moffat and learned the Tswana language. When Livingstone arrived, Moffat had already established a church and was translating the Bible into Tswana. It would be the first Bible translation in an indigenous southern African language.

Upon his arrival, Livingstone quickly established a rapport with the Africans. Although his somewhat raw and determined personality didn't always make him a favorite with Englishmen, Africans appreciated the respect he showed to them as equals and his ability to understand their customs and cultural thought processes.

The Moffats' oldest daughter Mary had been born in Africa, and Livingstone soon found that she shared his desire to reach the regions beyond established mission works. He proposed to her, and they married in 1845.

Shortly after their wedding, Livingstone and Mary moved further inland to open new mission stations for the gospel. Their final station was Kolobeng, Botswana—280 miles from the Moffats' work.

It was here that Livingstone's well-known attack by a lion occurred. Hearing villagers cry out for help from a lion who was stealing their sheep, Livingstone ran toward the lion with his rifle and shot it. The enraged and fatally-wounded lion caught Livingstone by his arm and shook him "as a terrier dog does a rat."[3] The strength of its jaws splintered his upper arm, and its teeth made gashes that left lifelong scars.

Providentially, Livingstone's African assistant Mebalwe—a faithful Christian man—appeared just then and again shot the lion. Mebalwe's gun misfired, and the lion released Livingstone and attacked Mebalwe. A second helper appeared and was also bitten before the lion died from Livingstone's original gunshot. All three men recovered, but Livingstone was marked for life. After attending to the other two, he had to set his

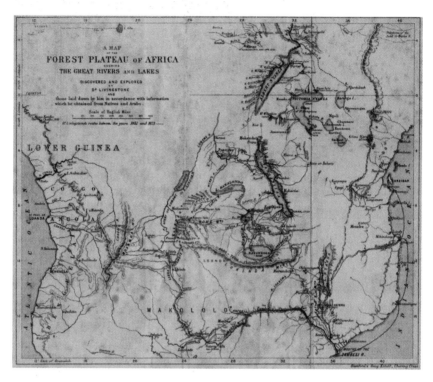

Map of Livingstone's Travels: This map, published in *The Last Journals of David Livingstone* (1874), charts the 28,000 miles he covered across central and southern Africa.

shattered arm himself (without the use of anesthesia). His shoulder would never be the same. For the rest of his life, he endured pain in it, most severely when he raised his arm.

Throughout these years, Livingstone remained preoccupied with the unevangelized areas of Africa. So many of the missionaries had settled around the coast towns. And although there was much gospel work to be done there, he couldn't escape the burden of the needs further in. Always, the interior called him. As he wrote home to his parents, he ended each letter with the question, "Who will penetrate the heart of Africa?"[4]

Livingstone made several evangelistic trips from his mission station, covering territory not yet touched by Europeans. In 1849, he went as far as Lake Ngami, almost 600 miles northeast of his home in Kolobeng. News of this journey and the "shimmering lake, some 80 miles long and 20 miles wide" made its way to England and was the beginning of his fame as an explorer. But more important to Livingstone were the national contacts he made in the area and the opportunities provided for him to share the gospel.

Two years later, Livingstone made another survey trip, this one further north and east, reaching the upper Zambezi River. Again, Livingstone was the first European to venture to the area. And again, he shared the gospel the entire way and longed to see missionaries established in these areas. Livingstone knew as well as anyone that, while itinerant preaching and witnessing were better than nothing, Africa would only be reached through consistent mission work, church planting, and Bible translation. And even as he prayed to see this realized, he sensed God leading him to forge ahead and provide reliable information that would open the way for the missionaries he prayed would come. At this time, not only was little of Africa known to any European, but even Africans themselves had little interest in what lay beyond their individual tribal regions. Livingstone felt that if he could fill in the map of Africa, missionaries would be more likely to come.

Furthermore, on Livingstone's two trips inland, he discovered the gut-wrenching cruelties of the slave trade being carried on throughout the interior. Even as he pushed through jungles no missionary had attempted, he would encounter Dutch or Portuguese slave traders with their captives chained together marching to the coast. As a first-hand witness to the cruelty and human suffering inflicted by this tragic evil, he could not help but want to do everything in his power to see it stopped. This further fueled his desire to open pathways for international trade through the continent, as he believed that access to legitimate trade in Africa's rich natural resources would expose and economically cripple the slave trade. Far from the idea of a colonialism for exploitation, his desire was to raise the standard of the oppressed.

In 1852, Livingstone and Mary came to the conclusion that he should embark on a multi-year expedition for a trade route from the center of southern Africa to the coast. The couple agreed that it would be best for the family's health and the children's education for Mary to take their five children back to England.

Livingstone sent three letters ahead of his family. He wrote to his father asking him to care for them. He wrote the London Missionary Society explaining his motives and purpose. And he wrote to his brother-in-law, "I shall open a path into the interior, or perish."[5]

Unlike the early Scottish martyrs, Livingstone wasn't an outsider because he held to the gospel itself under persecution. And yet, very like those great men and women, he was an outsider because of his love for the gospel. From this point on in Livingstone's life, he was determined to take the gospel to those who lived beyond the reach of current missionary work.

•   •   •   •   •

It's difficult, if not impossible, to overestimate the strength of Livingstone's will and perseverance.

Over the next three years, Livingstone traveled over *five thousand* miles through dense jungle and unexplored territory. He endured over thirty attacks of malaria and other African fevers, having to literally be carried part of the way because he was too weak to walk.

Most European explorers in Africa traveled in large caravans with dozens of soldiers and a litany of porters. Thus, locals often viewed them as a military intrusion or mistook them for slave raiders (literally, people who would come to a village and kidnap people to sell as slaves). In either case, the explorers were not well received.

Livingstone, however, traveled light, preferring to hunt or barter for meals on the way. He often had only African guides with him to help translate and carry the few supplies they brought. With his party of thirty or less people, he was more readily understood and respected than other explorers.

Livingstone began this three-year journey from Cape Town, on the southern tip of Africa, where he had first arrived twelve years prior, and traveled 1,500 miles northeast to Linyanti, Botswana, where Chief Sekeletu provided him with carriers and guides as well as ivory to trade on the journey.

From Linyanti, the group traveled another 1,500 miles northwest to the western coast town of Luanda, Angola. Livingstone arrived ill and exhausted. The trip had been eventful with his supplies stolen and some of his men deserting him. From the coast, he could have easily boarded a ship home, and many encouraged him to do so. But he refused for two reasons: he had promised Sekeletu's men that he would see them back to Linyanti, and he knew the difficult route he had traveled did not accomplish his objective of opening a highway for others. He decided to now travel to the east coast to see if he might find a better route.

Returning first to Linyanti, Livingstone then continued forward toward Mozambique. It was in this portion of the journey, that he came upon Victoria Falls. In the native language of Lozi, it was called "Mosi-oa-Tunya," or "the smoke that thunders," referring to its mist. He named it *Victoria Falls,* after his nation's queen. The falls were so immense that he wrote in his journal he couldn't possibly send the real size in his letters home, or he would lose credibility.

Everywhere Livingstone went, he encountered heathenism head on. He was a first-hand witness to the horrors of cannibalism and slave-raiding. He ached to see missionaries bring the gospel. How the question he had written to the London Missionary Society before he embarked on this journey must have burned in his mind: "Can the love of Christ not carry the missionary where the slave trade carries the trader?"[6]

Livingstone and his party reached Tete, Mozambique in March of 1856. He was disappointed that the medical supplies he had requested to be waiting for him were not there. He feared he had been forgotten, but the real reason the supplies hadn't been sent was even worse: no one had expected him to make it.

Although Livingstone wasn't the first to attempt a cross-continent journey, he was the first to actually accomplish it. During this trip, he mapped almost the entire course of the Zambezi River (missing only the section with the Cabora Bassa rapids, which would prove troublesome to him on his next journey). And he discovered two habitable elevations where he believed Europeans could live without getting malaria.

From Tete, Livingstone proceeded to Quelimane on the Mozambique coast and sailed home.

• • • • •

When Livingstone returned to Britain in 1856, he could not have anticipated the hero's welcome that awaited him.

The Royal Geographical Society gave him a gold medal, and the Universities of Oxford and Glasgow gave him honorary degrees. Churches, colleges, and every society imaginable invited him to speak. Livingstone used these opportunities to plead for missionaries for Africa. He spoke out against slavery and proposed European settlements to establish legitimate trade and teach Africans both scientific farming and international commerce.

When receiving his honorary Doctor of Laws degree at the University of Glasgow, he addressed the students. Gaunt, in poor health, his left arm crushed by a lion, he posed a question: "Would you like me to tell you what supported me through all the years of exile among a people whose language I could not understand, and whose attitude toward me was always uncertain and often hostile? It was this, 'Lo, I am with you alway, even unto the end of the world.' On these words I staked everything, and they never failed. I was never left alone."[7]

During Livingstone's expedition, he had kept a meticulous daily journal, writing even on the days he was too weak to travel. From these notes, he wrote and published *Missionary Travels* to awaken interest in missions in Africa. The book immediately sold out and had to be reprinted.

It was also during this furlough that Livingstone and the London Missionary Society mutually agreed for him to withdraw since he was no longer operating as a traditional missionary. Although he preached the gospel everywhere he went and had missionary objectives for his travels, he would in the future be funded by the Royal Geographical Society, his book sales, and even the Africans themselves.

Livingstone now prepared a new expedition to travel from the Mozambique coast up the Zambezi River to the interior, taking the route he proposed others travel. Sent out as the Queen's consul and funded by the Royal Geographical Society, Livingstone was forced to take a larger party than he preferred, including men accustomed to traveling as Europeans, and to use a large riverboat steamer. Livingstone would have preferred to travel lighter and use native African boats, but he determined to make the most of the opportunity he had, and he, Mary, and their son Oswell, once again sailed from England on March 10, 1858.

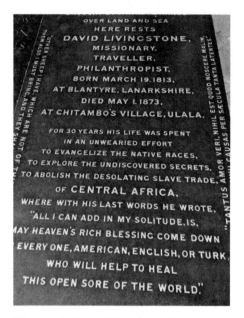

OVER LAND AND SEA
HERE RESTS
DAVID LIVINGSTONE,
MISSIONARY.
TRAVELLER.
PHILANTHROPIST.
BORN MARCH 19.1813,
AT BLANTYRE, LANARKSHIRE,
DIED MAY 1.1873,
AT CHITAMBO'S VILLAGE. ULALA.
FOR 30 YEARS HIS LIFE WAS SPENT
IN AN UNWEARIED EFFORT
TO EVANGELIZE THE NATIVE RACES,
TO EXPLORE THE UNDISCOVERED SECRETS,
TO ABOLISH THE DESOLATING SLAVE TRADE,
OF CENTRAL AFRICA,
WHERE WITH HIS LAST WORDS HE WROTE,
"ALL I CAN ADD IN MY SOLITUDE, IS,
MAY HEAVEN'S RICH BLESSING COME DOWN
EVERY ONE, AMERICAN, ENGLISH, OR TURK,
WHO WILL HELP TO HEAL
THIS OPEN SORE OF THE WORLD."

Livingstone's Grave in Westminster Abbey:
Livingstone was given all but a state funeral before being buried in one of the most prominent locations in Westminster Abbey. While Darwin and other notorious men rest on the side choir aisles, Livingstone is buried in the center of the nave, near the west entrance of the abbey.

On this expedition, Livingstone discovered Lake Nyasa and explored both the Shire and Rovuma Rivers. He assisted in establishing sites for missions, preached the gospel, provided medical help, and contributed scientific and missionary articles for periodicals in England. He exposed the atrocities of the slave trade, shocking the world with the evil he was seeing firsthand.

During this journey, Mary, who had returned to England and then rejoined her husband, died after three months of fever.

Livingstone was crushed. He wrote home to comfort his children . . . and wrote in his own journal, "For the first time in my life, I want to die."

But God still had work for Livingstone to accomplish.

• • • • •

Other than its benefit of proving what could not be done, the Zambezi expedition was disappointing in every way. The large steamer continually leaked. The European men with Livingstone chaffed under his stubborn determination. It's hard to say how much of their negative reports of Livingstone were accurate and how much were a reaction to being held to his standard of endurance. One biographer explained it this way: "It was the very greatness of his views, the boundlessness of their range, that made it impossible for some people to understand him. He felt this keenly, and was led to explain in a half-apologetic, half-independent strain. 'We are working hard,' he writes to his mother, 'at what some can see at a glance the importance of, while to others we appear to be following after the glory of discovering lakes, mountains, jenny-nettles and puddock-stools.'"[8]

When the party reached the section of the Zambezi which Livingstone had previously missed, they discovered the Cabora Bassa rapids, which brought an end to Livingstone's dream of using the Zambezi as a water highway through the continent. One of the men with him reported that as he reached a thirty-foot waterfall, Livingstone waved his hand as if to wish it away and said, "That's not supposed to be there."

The British government, "which had no interest in forcing steamers up cataracts," recalled Livingstone and his mission party.[9] He returned to England defeated and disappointed but more determined than ever to find another route.

During this his final trip to England, where he was reunited with his mother and children, Livingstone wrote and published *Narrative of an Expedition to the Zambezi and Its Tributaries*. It did not sell as well as his first book, but it did help fund his final journey.

Livingstone now turned his face once again toward Africa, hoping to end her double scourge of sin and slavery. His stated purpose for what would be his final expedition was to go inland, north of the Portuguese slave traders to open this area for missions. He also wanted to understand the watershed of this region in Africa and specifically hoped to find the source for the Nile River.

• • • • •

Livingstone's final journey was his most difficult. He was fifty-three years old and had spent much of the past twenty-five years pushing his body beyond its physical limits. His guides deserted him and falsely reported that he was dead. His medicines were stolen twice, and he was constantly ill with one or a combination of malaria, pneumonia, tropical ulcers on his feet, and cholera.

Adding to his difficulties, Livingstone's work in exposing the slave trade had made him enemies of the Arab and Portuguese traders through whose territory he was seeking to pass. Although at points on this journey he was forced to rely on their aid due to his sicknesses, they constantly thwarted his efforts, including refusing to carry his dispatches. (Only one of his final forty-four letters made it out of Africa.)

Even so, this trip was full of discoveries. Livingstone did not find the source of the Nile as he had hoped, but he did discover Lake Bangweulu and the Lualaba River, which he realized flows into the Congo, rather than the Nile. It was an important discovery in terms of understanding Africa's waterways.

While on the banks of the Lualaba, Livingstone witnessed the massacre of about four hundred Africans by slave traders. This incident shattered an already-frail Livingstone, and he could not find the emotional strength to go forward. He returned the 240 miles to the nearest Arab settlement of Ujiji, violently ill most of the way.

It was while Livingstone was recovering in Ujiji that the news reporter Henry Stanley showed up and uttered the now famous words, "Dr. Livingstone, I presume?" Stanley arrived in November of 1871 and stayed with Livingstone for a few months, writing home, "I challenge any man to find a fault in his character. . . . The secret is that his religion is a constant, earnest and sincere practice."[10]

Livingstone was greatly refreshed by Stanley's arrival as well as the letters he brought with him. For four months he and Stanley explored the nearby Lake Tanganyika. When Stanley left, he pleaded with Livingstone to come with him, but Livingstone was determined to return to his objective of finding the source for the Nile. He did, however, ask Stanley for a favor—to bring Livingstone's journals

Westminster Abbey: Although Livingstone's body was buried here in Westminster Abbey with the kings and queens of Great Britain, his heart was buried under a Baobab tree in central Africa.

and letters out with him. (One letter included was to the editor of the *New York Herald,* the newspaper which had sent Stanley. In it, Livingstone wrote, "And if my disclosures regarding the terrible Ujijian slavery should lead to the suppression of the East Coast slave trade, I shall regard that as a greater matter by far than the discovery of all the Nile sources together."[11]

For the next thirteen months, Livingstone soldiered on. Although renewed by Stanley's visit, physically he was more ill than ever. Plagued with dysentery and fever, he had to be carried most of the way, always in excruciating pain.

When his party reached the village of Ilala, in modern-day Zambia, Livingstone was suffering internal bleeding from the dysentery and wracked with fever from malaria. In this greatly weakened condition he drew maps of the area they had just covered and painstakingly updated his journal with his observations of the territory.

On May 1, 1873, Livingstone's two faithful servants, Chuma and Susi, who had been with him through this entire expedition, found Livingstone's body kneeling before his bed. His spirit had already gone to be with the Lord.

What happened next gives us a poignant glimpse into the high esteem in which the Africans held David Livingstone. Recognizing Livingstone to be a great man in his country, Chuma and Susi determined that his body must be sent back to England. They buried his heart and his organs under a Baobab tree, but they dried his body in the sun and then proceeded to carry it (along with his recent journals) on a nine-month, thousand-mile journey to the coast and then accompanied it to England.

In England, Livingstone's body was verified by the upper arm which had been crushed by the lion so many years previous, and he was buried in Westminster Abbey.

Livingstone's split burial—his body in Westminster Abbey and his heart in Africa—is a fitting tribute to his life.

● ● ● ● ●

As an explorer, Livingstone gave his life to open the deep interior of the dark continent of Africa. On his journeys he had covered 28,000 miles, crossing Africa from west to east and following the waterways to the sources of the Congo.

As a missionary, Livingstone preached the gospel in hundreds of African villages. Although he saw little direct fruit from his labor, he couldn't have known of the fruit that would come in the generations to follow. The missionaries on African soil today are there largely because of the sacrifices Livingstone made to follow Christ through unknown paths, staggering on through fever, loneliness, and even abandonment.

Livingstone's own views on his sacrifices, however, are humbling and convicting. May they challenge you—as they do me—to more wholehearted service to the Lord:

> People talk of the sacrifice I have made in spending so much of my life in Africa. Can that be called a sacrifice which is simply paid back as a small part of a great debt owing to our God, which we can never repay? Is that a sacrifice which brings its own blest reward in healthful activity, the consciousness of doing good, peace of mind, and a bright hope of a glorious destiny hereafter? Away with the word in such a view, and with such a thought! It is emphatically no sacrifice. Say rather it is a privilege. Anxiety, sickness, suffering, or danger, now and then, with a foregoing of the common conveniences and charities of this life, may make us pause, and cause the spirit to waver, and the soul to sink, but let this only be for a moment. All these are nothing when compared with the glory which shall hereafter be revealed in, and for, us. I never made a sacrifice. Of this we ought not to talk, when we remember the great sacrifice which He made who left His Father's throne on high to give Himself for us.[12]

TRUTHS FOR OUTSIDERS

What do we learn from the life of David Livingstone?

God directs the steps of those yielded to Him. Considering all that Livingstone did in Africa, it's amazing to realize that he originally planned to be a missionary in China. Proverbs 16:9 applies to David Livingstone's life: "A man's heart deviseth his way: but the Lord directeth his steps." God ordered Livingstone's steps in this redirection, as He did throughout Livingstone's travels in Africa, through the needs and opportunities in front of him.

Sometimes we worry about *where* God's will is more than *what* His will is. Although Livingstone did not serve as a missionary in the location he originally planned, he carried the gospel across a continent. Had he grown discouraged in waiting during the Opium War and given up on missions, he never would have opened the interior of Africa to missions, and millions of lives would have been affected.

See the need, take the lead. Surely Livingstone wasn't the first missionary to notice that missions work in Africa was clustered around the coasts. Neither was he the first to realize there was a continent of people without so much as the opportunity to hear of Christ. But Livingstone was no armchair philosopher theorizing how missions might change if someone found ways to penetrate inland. As he so succinctly said, "Sympathy is no substitute for action." Has God drawn your attention to needs around you? What could you do toward meeting those needs?

To make a difference for God, persevere. Livingstone faced one setback or reversal after another, and at any step of the way, he could have given in to discouragement and defeat. When his dream of using the Zambezi as a water highway was crushed at the Cabora Bassa rapids, he could have given up. When he realized the river he was following was not part of the Nile water system as he had thought, he could have given up. When those who once praised him now criticized him, he could have given up. When he was so sick he could not walk and then had his medicines stolen by those who deserted him and reported him dead, he could have given up. When he saw few converts and gruesome scenes of human suffering, he could have given up. But Livingstone didn't give up. He endured criticism, mutiny, hunger, sickness, and fear. And his dogged perseverance opened up an entire continent to the gospel of Jesus Christ.

Our legacy is not only what we accomplish, but is also in whom we influence. News of Livingstone's death reached a young Scottish girl named Mary Slessor. And she was convinced that God wanted her to give her life to Africa. She sailed for Nigeria in 1876, and her work there bore great fruit. In addition to spreading the gospel, Mary helped put an end to the practice of killing twins at birth (as the locals believed twins to be a curse). After Mary had been on the field for some time, visiting friends from Scotland expressed amazement at what she had been able to accomplish in the face of such great obstacles. One of the converted native chiefs who was listening to the conversation responded, "You speak only of what the woman has accomplished. You have clearly forgotten to think of the woman's God."

Although Livingstone's geological achievements were great, his impact on people, such as Mary Slessor, was profoundly greater. Only God knows and only eternity will reveal how many people have been and will be impacted through David Livingstone's example and influence.

CHARLES SPURGEON
(1834–1892)

"A sermon without Christ in it is like a loaf of bread without any
flour in it. No Christ in your sermon, sir? Then go home, and
never preach again until you have something worth preaching."

Charles Spurgeon

Over the years, the Lord has given our church the
opportunity to hear from some of the great preachers of
His Word, including many men now in Heaven such as
Dr. Curtis Hutson, Dr. Tom Malone, Dr. Lee Roberson,
and others.

I remember as a young pastor feeling inadequate to even introduce
these visiting preachers to our church family. I wanted to make sure to
honor these great men by accurately describing their faithfulness to the
Lord and what God had done through them, and I wanted our church
family to love them as much as I did.

That intimidation is a little how I feel in introducing Charles
Spurgeon to you. Remembered today as the "Prince of Preachers,"

Spurgeon preached more than 3,600 times and to weekly crowds of over six thousand people. His messages were drenched in Scripture and keenly applied to the common man in nineteenth century London.

In Spurgeon's lifetime, his printed sermons sold at a rate of 25,000 copies weekly and, in the course of his forty-year ministry, over 56,000,000 copies sold in nearly forty languages. To this day, Spurgeon remains the most quoted preacher. In fact, not many weeks pass without a quote from Spurgeon in my own sermons.

But Spurgeon was more than his sermons. He was a man who knew God and His Word and committed his life to share both with his generation. Thankfully, God has used him to touch our generation as well.

•　•　•　•　•

Charles Spurgeon was born on June 19, 1834, in Kelvedon, Essex, in England. He was born into a long line of preachers, with both his father and grandfather pastoring as Spurgeon grew up.

When Spurgeon was eighteen months old, he was sent to live with his father's parents in Stambourne, twenty miles away. The reason for this is not recorded, but all evidence indicates it was due to economic strain in his immediate family.

In any case, Spurgeon loved the five years he spent with his grandparents in their tiny English village. It was here that his eighteen-year-old aunt Anne taught him to read, and he developed his lifelong love for books. His grandfather-pastor owned a remarkably large library, and Spurgeon spent hours in it. His brother James once said that Charles "used to read about everything, with a memory as tenacious as a vice and as copious as a barn."[1] Even as a boy, he saturated his mind with great books written by some of God's most devoted servants. He read *Pilgrim's Progress* for the first time when he was six—and he reread it at least one hundred times throughout his life.

Another favorite of Spurgeon's was *Foxe's Book of Martyrs*. Even as a boy, he knew that he came from a long line of outsiders. With both his father and grandfather serving as pastors of dissenter churches (any congregation not part of the Church of England), Spurgeon was well-aware of the rich heritage he shared with previous martyrs of the faith. John Huss, Patrick Hamilton, Hugh Latimer, Nicolas Ridley, John Bunyan, and other such men were Spurgeon's childhood heroes. Their stories indelibly impressed on his heart the value of strong, biblical convictions.

Spurgeon's grandfather would often host traveling preachers, and Spurgeon loved to listen to their theological debates. His sharp mind soaked in and retained everything he heard. (He later recalled one of these debates having to do with believer's baptism. Spurgeon's family were Congregationalists and practiced infant baptism. Even at a young age, Spurgeon found the arguments for infant baptism weak.) Between the Puritan authors he read in his grandfather's study and the conversations to which he listened, even as a child Spurgeon developed an immense store of theological knowledge and began forming personal biblical convictions. In a sermon many years later, he described an early churchman of England who had no backbone this way: "The gross example of the Vicar of Bray comes at once to one's mind, who had been a papist under Henry VIII, then a protestant under a Protestant reign, then a papist under Mary, then again a Protestant under Elizabeth; and he declared he had always been consistent with his principle, for his principle was to continue as the Vicar of Bray."[2] Spurgeon knew no such vascillation. He early developed biblical principles and remained true to them throughout his life, even when it became costly.

When Spurgeon's father took a new church in Colchester, Spurgeon moved back home. But he missed his grandparents and his aunt and returned every summer to visit. Years later, when Spurgeon was London's most popular pastor, he continued to return to Stambourne where he found a sanctuary from the demands of the city and the pressures of critics.

Remarkably, Spurgeon didn't trust Christ as his personal Saviour until he was fifteen years old. Perhaps even more remarkable is that his salvation was preceded by a spiritual crisis. Although he knew the doctrines of justification and understood Christ's substitutionary atonement, he couldn't bring himself to a point of simple faith. He believed *in* Christ, but he had not believed *on* Christ; and for some reason, he couldn't seem to separate the two.

For months, Spurgeon privately agonized under the Holy Spirit's conviction. By all outward appearances, he was a model Christian. He had attended church multiple times a week, walked great distances to hear traveling preachers, and lived a clean life. But he couldn't shake the sense of guilt over his sin . . . and at the same time refused to give up his sense of self-sufficiency.

This all came to a head one Sunday morning in January when Spurgeon got caught in a snowstorm on his way to a church his mother had told him about. Bitterly cold, he stepped into a Primitive Methodist chapel and sat near the back of the mostly-empty sanctuary.

The pastor didn't show up, presumably not able to make it through the storm. But at last, a man from the congregation agreed to share a message and chose Isaiah 45:22 for his text, "Look unto me, and be ye saved, all the ends of the earth: for I am God, and there is none else."

Spurgeon later related: "He was obliged to stick to his text, for the simple reason that he had little else to say. . . . He did not even pronounce the words rightly, but that did not matter. There was, I thought, a glimmer of hope for me in that text."

After the preacher labored on for some ten minutes, repeating "Look unto me," again and again as he described Christ's death and resurrection, he turned his attention to the one guest present. Spurgeon wrote, "he looked at me under the gallery, and . . . Just fixing his eyes on me, as if he knew all my heart, he said, 'Young man, you look very miserable.' Well, I did, but I had not been accustomed to have remarks made from the pulpit on my personal appearance before. However, it was a good blow, struck right home. He continued, 'And you will always be miserable—miserable in life and miserable in death—if you do not obey my text; but if you obey now, this moment, you will be saved.'"

Suddenly Spurgeon understood salvation—not the theological doctrine alone, but the practical application—that he, Charles Spurgeon, had only to personally look in faith to what Christ had already done for him. "I saw at once the way of salvation . . . . I had been waiting to do fifty things, but when I heard that word, 'Look!' . . . Oh! I looked until I could almost have looked my eyes away."[3]

Spurgeon looked to Christ, and he would never be the same—nor would England. Nor would the rest of the world.

• • • • •

Perhaps the most immediate evidence of anyone's salvation is their desire to see others saved. And this proved true in Spurgeon's life. Biographer Richard Day recorded, "The very next day found him visiting the poor and talking to his classmates concerning their religious life; and heard him declare to his teacher, Mr. Swindell, 'It's all settled; I must preach the gospel of Christ.' Notwithstanding his previous unimpeachable character, all his friends and acquaintances recognized the great transformation."[4]

After Spurgeon's salvation, he returned to the question of believer's baptism he had heard debated as a child. Convinced that the New Testament definitely taught baptism by immersion after salvation, he determined to be baptized. At the time, he was living in Newmarket, assisting in a school and attending classes himself, so he wrote to his parents to inform them of his conviction and ask their blessing.

Spurgeon's mother returned a less than enthusiastic reply: "Ah, Charles, I have often prayed the Lord to make you a Christian, but I never asked that you might become a Baptist." In his reply, we see something of the humor that would color his sermons in years to come: "Ah, Mother, the Lord has answered your prayer with His usual bounty, and has given you exceeding abundantly above what you asked or thought."[5] He was baptized on his mother's birthday, May 3, 1850, just a few weeks before his own sixteenth birthday.

Spurgeon remained a Baptist throughout his life. Some years later, as he addressed a group of Baptist preachers, he pointed out that Baptists have held to the distinctives of New Testament local churches since the churches of the first century.

> We believe that the Baptists are the original Christians. We did not commence our existence at the reformation, we were reformers before Luther or Calvin were born; we never came from the Church of Rome, for we were never in it, but we have an unbroken line up to the apostles themselves. We have always existed from the very days of Christ, and our principles, sometimes veiled and forgotten, like a river which may travel

underground for a little season, have always had honest and holy adherents. Persecuted alike by Romanists and Protestants of almost every sect, yet there has never existed a Government holding Baptist principles which persecuted others; nor I believe any body of Baptists ever held it to be right to put the consciences of others under the control of man. We have ever been ready to suffer, as our martyrologies will prove, but we are not ready to accept any help from the State, to prostitute the purity of the Bride of Christ to any alliance with the government, and we will never make the Church, although the Queen, the despot over the consciences of men.[6]

Metropolitan Tabernacle: Spurgeon insisted that his church's new building include Greek columns because the New Testament was written in Greek. The church continues as a gospel-preaching Baptist church in London to this day.

At fifteen years of age, Spurgeon continued his witnessing efforts, spending his Saturdays giving out gospel tracts and seeking opportunities to speak to people about the Lord. He also began teaching Sunday school and soon found several adults sitting in to listen to his clear, relatable Bible teaching.

A few months later, Spurgeon moved to the city of Cambridge and joined St. Andrew's Street Baptist Church. Within a short time, James Vinter, the leader of the church's preaching ministry to nearby villages, recruited Spurgeon to help.

At a mere sixteen years old, Spurgeon preached his first sermon in a thatched-roof cottage in Teversham, England. His message was a simple

Spurgeon's Pulpit: The Metropolitan Tabernacle continues to honor the legacy of Charles Spurgeon. Pictured at left here is the church's current pastor (since 1970), Peter Masters.

salvation message, but his manner in presenting it was clear and reached the hearts of his hearers.

Spurgeon preached the next week in another village. And the next in another. Soon, he was preaching multiple times a week.

One Sunday he preached at the Baptist church in the village of Waterbeach. The congregation asked him to return the next Sunday. On the third Sunday, they asked him to be their regular pastor. He was just seventeen years old.

It was at Waterbeach where Spurgeon personally led his first soul to Christ. He saw this as God's seal of blessing on his ministry. It was also at Waterbeach that Spurgeon published his first printed work—a gospel tract.

When Spurgeon became pastor at Waterbeach, the church had a congregation of about forty, but it soon grew rapidly as people came from all over the village and the surrounding villages to hear the boy preacher as he opened God's Word to them with wisdom, insight, power, and maturity. His years of exposure to God's Word and the great theological truths from his grandfather's books had worked their way into his heart and mind and now worked their way out into his messages. Soon, the church was full every Sunday, with people standing outside listening through the open windows.

But more than a crowd on Sundays, Waterbeach itself went through a transformation. The village was notorious for drunkenness and debauchery, but as Spurgeon faithfully preached, he found that the gospel is indeed "the power of God unto salvation" (Romans 1:16). Soon, the gambling dens closed, and from nearly every thatched roof at sundown, came sounds of families singing hymns in worship. Years later Spurgeon wrote that God "made me a witness of that Gospel which can win souls, draw reluctant hearts, and mould afresh the life and conduct of sinful men and women."[7]

Two years after Spurgeon began his pastorate in Waterbeach, however, he received an invitation he never would have expected—to preach for New Park Street Baptist Chapel in London in view of becoming their pastor.

• • • • •

New Park Street Baptist Chapel had an illustrious history. Started in 1650 (about the same time Bunyan began preaching in Bedford), the church had survived the tumultuous, persecution-filled years when dissenters were forbidden from meeting. In 1688, when a measure of religious freedom was available, the church built its first building near the tower bridge area of London. From 1720–1836, the church had two pastors, Dr. John Gill and Dr. John Rippon, who served fifty-one and sixty-three years, respectively. Under their faithful leadership, the church flourished. In 1833, Dr. Rippon led the church in moving to New Park Street where they erected and filled weekly a 1,200-seat building.

Over the next two decades, however, London itself shifted, leaving New Park Street in a dense, often-flooded, inner city area from which much of the congregation moved out. The church dwindled in size so that by the time the deacons invited Spurgeon to preach, there were only two hundred on the membership rolls and considerably less in attendance.

The recorded minutes from a church meeting on December 14, 1853, just four days before Spurgeon preached his first sermon there, offer insight into difficulties the church faced: "Dear Brethren, We regret that, during the past year, we have made no additions to our numbers in consequence of our being without a Pastor." The minutes, which were sent to the London Baptist Association, closed with these revealing words: "We enclose our statistics. Brethren, pray for us."[8]

On the first Sunday Spurgeon preached, the large auditorium was almost empty.

In London for the first time, Spurgeon was obviously out of place—a village boy in one of Europe's greatest cities. He found, in fact, that he hated London with its noise and pollution and the signs of human misery everywhere he looked. He was intimidated, too, by the greatness of the church at which he was to preach. He had never preached in one so large, not to mention respected and influential, and was dreadfully nervous. His appearance, mannerisms, and strong accent betrayed him as something of a country bumpkin.

But when Spurgeon opened God's Word and began his sermon, the small congregation was amazed. They could not have anticipated

St. Andrews Street Baptist Church, Cambridge: This is the church from which Spurgeon first began preaching at age fifteen. My grandson, Camden, is standing by the Lord's Table.

the depth of maturity or insight, the clarity in presentation, and the relatability of Spurgeon's style.

When nineteen-year-old Spurgeon returned to the pulpit that evening, the congregation had swelled.

Two weeks later, the deacons asked Spurgeon to be their pastor. He was not yet twenty years old, and he was on the brink of pastoring what had been one of London's largest churches.

● ● ● ● ●

Seated in the congregation that first Sunday night Spurgeon preached at New Park Street Baptist was the young Susannah Thompson. A cultured Londoner, she was a little amused and a little put off by his countrified appearance and accent and not especially impressed that he was to be the church's new pastor.

Baptist Church in Waterbeach: Years after Spurgeon's first pastorate in Waterbeach, England, the church needed to build again. Spurgeon himself laid the foundation stone for this current building in 1863.

Four months later, however, when Susannah shared with her cousin and her husband, Susannah and William Olney, the doubts she was struggling with concerning her salvation, William must have shared them with their new pastor. For soon after, Susannah was surprised to receive an illustrated copy of *Pilgrim's Progress* with a note on the flyleaf: "Miss Thompson, with desires for her progress in the blessed pilgrimage. From C. H. Spurgeon, April 20, 1854."⁹

Spurgeon's care for Susannah was something more than pastoral. Over the following few months, a friendship blossomed. Spurgeon proposed in August, and they were married on January 8, 1856. Almost a year later, Susannah gave birth to their only children, twin sons named Charles and Thomas. Charles and Susannah's almost four-decade marriage was one of deep love for each other, shared love for Christ, and joy in serving Him as a family.

But it wasn't only Spurgeon's personal life that flourished. New Park Street Baptist experienced immediate and exponential growth under their new pastor and his biblical, practical, and incredibly relatable preaching. Spurgeon spoke to the common man. He didn't use pompous language, and he didn't speak to impress theologians. With God's enablement, he preached to reach hearts.

Spurgeon labored diligently over his messages. He often wrote the entire message out before he preached, but he only carried the simple outline into the pulpit with him.

Less than a year after Spurgeon became the pastor of New Park Street Baptist, a publisher and member of the church invited him to begin printing his sermons in the newspaper. The first was printed in January of 1855, and it continued weekly until after Spurgeon's death. It was in these early years that he also began his writing ministry, eventually averaging four books a year (mostly compiled from his preached messages) for a total of some 140 titles.

With the exploding growth of Spurgeon's ministry came heavy criticism—a common plight of leaders who live outside the traditions of men. The media accused him of being a mere entertainer, a sensationalist. Cartoonists mocked Spurgeon's appearance. Other pastors, jealous and perhaps frustrated at their own declining ministries, accused him of being a boy wonder, an inexperienced youth who would soon fade into oblivion. They critiqued his down-to-earth preaching style and everyday language as "vulgar."

Spurgeon didn't bother to answer these criticisms (except to write his parents when there were attacks on his character, assuring them they were untrue), but he felt them keenly. Susannah kept every defaming news article and put them in a scrapbook. She also hung a framed copy

Auckland Baptist Tabernacle: The Spurgeons' son, Thomas, pastored this church until his father's death, at which time the deacons of the Metropolitan Tabernacle called him to be their pastor. His twin brother, Charles, pastored the Greenwich Baptist Church.

of Matthew 5:11–12 on the wall: "Blessed are ye, when men shall revile you, and persecute you, and shall say all manner of evil against you falsely, for my sake. Rejoice, and be exceeding glad: for great is your reward in heaven: for so persecuted they the prophets which were before you."

By February of 1854, the church's 1,200-seat auditorium was overcrowded and turning people away. The church temporarily moved services to Exeter Hall while they renovated to add 300 seats.

Exeter seated four thousand with standing room for an additional one thousand, but it, too, was soon filled to capacity. When the church tried to move back into their newly-renovated auditorium, they immediately realized they had built too small. They then made plans to relocate where they could build a new auditorium.

Spurgeon and the deacons chose an empty piece of property at Elephant and Castle, near the River Thames and close to the church's original location of the seventeenth century. They specifically chose the site of the 1557 burning of the Southwark Martyrs under Queen Mary's rule for their new building. The church's foundation stone includes the inscription, "The blood of the martyrs is the seed of the church," in honor of the men who gave their lives there.

While the new building was under construction, the church had no choice but to again look for a temporary location. They chose the largest indoor venue in London—the ten-thousand-seat Surrey Gardens Music Hall. It was here that tragedy struck.

• • • • •

There are moments that mark one for life. Such was October 9, 1856 for Spurgeon—the church's first Sunday service at Surrey Hall.

As Spurgeon began his message, the ten-thousand-seat auditorium was full, with thousands having been turned away. Pranksters in the back yelled out, "Fire!" and "The galleries are falling!" Pandemonium led to stampede, and before it was over, seven people were trampled to their deaths with twenty-eight others seriously wounded.

When Spurgeon understood what had happened, he physically collapsed. Over the next several days, he remained in a state of shocked grief. Susannah wrote, "My beloved's anguish was so deep and violent, that reason seemed to totter in her throne, and we sometimes feared that he would never preach again."[10]

But Spurgeon did preach again. Just two weeks later, he returned to Surrey Hall and spoke to his congregation of God's sustaining grace.

This tragedy never left Spurgeon. It seemed to be at least a partial source of the seasons of depression he would endure for the remainder of his life. But as deep as the pain had been was the deepening of his empathy. Spurgeon now preached with a compassion and sympathy that often marks the ministries of those who endure profound suffering. He had drunk more deeply of God's grace, and his preaching more fully carried its richness.

For the next four and a half years, the church continued to meet in Surrey Hall until the dedication service of the Metropolitan Tabernacle on March 31, 1861. Spurgeon was still only twenty-six years old.

• • • • •

Accepting invitations from other churches, Spurgeon often preached as many as ten times each week. And still, he found time for other ministries.

In 1857, Spurgeon began the Pastor's College to train men who were called to ministry. Spurgeon himself had not had the opportunity of ministerial training, but he believed it could be a great help. "Every man regrets," he said, "when in the field that he did not prepare better before he entered it."[11] His book *Lectures to My Students*, birthed out of his Friday afternoon class in the Pastor's College, was one of the first books I received as a Bible college student and is a favorite of mine.

Graduates of the Pastor's College were numerous and fruitful. Within the first twelve years, they were responsible for planting dozens of new churches and baptizing a collective total of 39,000 new converts.[9] The college would eventually train over nine hundred graduates in Spurgeon's lifetime.

Students from the Pastor's College joined members from Spurgeon's church in inner city ministry, often going to the slums of London with warm food and a gospel message. Under Spurgeon's direction, they started extension chapels throughout the poorest areas of the city.

When Spurgeon first arrived in London, his heart was broken by the needs of the street children lying starving in the gutters. Strengthened by

Olive Orchard in Mentone, France: When Spurgeon was in Mentone, he would often come here to pray.

the example of George Müller in Bristol, the Metropolitan Tabernacle opened the Stockwell Orphanage. They also opened seventeen almshouses for the poor as well as a day school for children. As Spurgeon told his congregation, "We are a large church, and we must have a large heart for this city."[12]

Spurgeon used his sermon and book sales to fund large portions of the ministries in which he was involved as well as to send generous gifts to other ministries, including George Müller's orphanages in Bristol and Hudson Taylor's mission in China.

Printed copies of Spurgeon's sermons found their way around the world. Eventually a worn and tattered copy made its way back to Spurgeon. At the top of the first page was a handwritten note: "Very good, D. L." David Livingstone had carried this sermon with him through his final journeys in Africa, and it was found among his few possessions after his death in 1873. It was mailed to Spurgeon and became a great treasure to him.

When the Metropolitan Tabernacle was officially finished and the congregation held its first Sunday services there, the crowds continued to pour in. The Tabernacle could seat five thousand people, with standing room for an additional one thousand, and it filled weekly with the streets nearby gridlocked with horse-drawn carriages from the early hours of Sunday mornings as people came to hear Spurgeon.

Queen Victoria herself requested that Spurgeon preach at the Crystal Palace for the national day of humiliation and prayer after the Indian Mutiny of 1857. With 23,654 people in attendance, Spurgeon preached a clear gospel message without a microphone or any mechanical amplification.

A couple days before the event, Spurgeon went to test the acoustics and lifted his voice with the text John 1:29, "Behold the Lamb of God, which taketh away the sin of the world." A workman in the gallery heard it, put down his tools, and trusted Christ as his Saviour.

The stories of others saved directly and indirectly through Spurgeon's preaching and witness are numerous. It is said that one woman was converted through reading a single page of one of his sermons wrapped around some butter she had bought.

Spurgeon continued his labor as a soulwinner, making personal visits to homes. He also made himself available on Monday mornings for anyone who had had attended services on Sunday and had questions about their salvation.

Throughout his life, Spurgeon suffered much physical pain from rheumatism, gout, neuritis, and Bright's disease (a burning kidney inflammation). Additionally, he continued to experience seasons of mental and emotional pain in depression. Overwork and constant stress did not help his health. In time, he began spending three or four of the winter months in Mentone, France, where the balmy Mediterranean breezes and respite from the rigors of his London schedule eased some of the pain and braced him for another season of ministry.

* * * * *

In March of 1887, Spurgeon published an article titled "The Down-Grade" in his monthly paper, *The Sword and the Trowel*. The article was credited to an anonymous author but was written by Spurgeon's friend, Robert Shindler. It described the downgrading of doctrine that was taking place in evangelical churches as a result of the liberalism and higher criticism that was sweeping Europe. Specifically, the author was concerned that even Baptist pastors were denying such essential doctrines as the deity of Christ and salvation through His substitutionary death.

A few months later, Spurgeon himself wrote an article on the same subject titled "Another Word Concerning the Down-Grade." In it, he not only laid out the necessity of doctrinal integrity and absolute adherence

Mentone, France: Although Mentone is often warm and sunny, on the day we visited it was overcast. It was easy to imagine a burdened, pain-ridden Spurgeon coming here for rest and time to renew his soul in God.

to biblical authority, but he also raised the question of ecclesiastical separation from those who were not willing to clearly contend for the faith.

> It now becomes a serious question how far those who abide by the faith once delivered to the saints should fraternize with those who have turned aside to another gospel. Christian love has its claims, and divisions are to be shunned as grievous evils; but how far are we justified in being in confederacy with those who are departing from the truth? It is a difficult question to answer so as to keep the balance of the duties. For the present it behooves believers to be cautious, lest they lend their support and countenance to the betrayers of the Lord. . . . Let each believer judge for himself; but, for our part, we have put on a few fresh bolts to our door, and we have given orders to keep the chain up; for, under colour of begging the friendship of the servant, there are those about who aim at robbing the Master.[13]

The Baptist Union, of which the Metropolitan Tabernacle had been a part since before Spurgeon became its pastor, bristled at his strong words. The reality was that within the Baptist Union there *were* liberal pastors denying foundational doctrines of Scripture.

The Down-Grade Controversy, as it came to be called, raged for some time. Spurgeon continued to write on the necessity of orthodox doctrine, and the Baptist Union, which surprisingly had no statement of faith for its members, became divided over the issue. Their refusal to take a stand against liberalism and their willingness to allow known liberals to continue in the group greatly troubled Spurgeon.

Finally, in October of 1887, Spurgeon determined he must, as the godly outsiders of his heritage had done, stand as an outsider on this issue as well. With a commitment to orthodox doctrine, Spurgeon graciously and quietly withdrew from the Baptist Union.

Embarrassed at losing their most influential member, the Baptist Union wouldn't let the matter drop. They met in January of 1888 to hold an official vote of censure of Spurgeon, accusing him of stirring controversy and false accusations. This rejection and, especially, his continuing concern over pastors leaving the faith, caused deep grief for Spurgeon.

Looking back, God undoubtedly used Spurgeon's faithfulness to "contend for the faith which was once delivered unto the saints" (Jude 3) to prevent the further spread of liberalism in England. (In the coming decades, the English Baptists did not capitulate to liberalism as other denominations across Europe did.) But for Spurgeon, his stand was costly. His health so deteriorated and then quickly declined over this time period that Susannah later wrote, "his fight for the faith . . . cost him his life."[14]

Spurgeon's Grave: Charles and Susannah Spurgeon are buried in West Norwood Cemetery in London. The marble Bible on his grave is inscribed with the words of 2 Timothy 4:7–8, "I have fought a good fight, I have finished my course, I have kept the faith: Henceforth there is laid up for me a crown of righteousness, which the Lord, the righteous judge, shall give me at that day: and not to me only, but unto all them also that love his appearing."

• • • • •

On June 7, 1891, Spurgeon preached what would prove to be his last sermon at Metropolitan Tabernacle. That very week, he found himself bedridden in pain and illness he had been fighting for months. In

October, Charles and Susannah followed the doctor's orders to go to Mentone, France, where it was hoped that the warmth, sunshine, and sea air would restore his health.

Initially, Spurgeon rallied, even writing his final book (an exposition of the Gospel of Matthew) during the first few months there. But in January of 1892, he took a turn for the worse.

On Sunday night, January 31, 1892, Spurgeon went to be with His Lord. His body was transported back to London for a funeral at the Metropolitan Tabernacle.

Spurgeon's funeral filled London. The church held a week of services to make room for all who wanted to attend, with each day designated for a different group of people. Over one hundred thousand people lined the streets as Spurgeon's body was taken to the cemetery after the last service.

It is estimated that Spurgeon preached to ten million people in his lifetime. Since his death, his words have continued to touch the lives of countless millions through his printed sermons and books. And perhaps, he still preaches. After all, he used to say that once in Heaven he "would stand at the corner of one of the streets and proclaim to the angels the old, old story of Jesus and His love."[15] That's not hard to believe, since it would be but a continuation of what he did his entire life.

TRUTHS FOR OUTSIDERS

What do we learn from the life of Charles Spurgeon?

Christ's last command must be our first priority. Spurgeon's earliest efforts in serving the Lord were not in preaching, but in soulwinning. Four months after his salvation, he wrote his parents, "I have seventy people whom I regularly visit on Saturday. I do not give a tract and go away, but I sit down and endeavor to draw their attention to spiritual realities . . . I trust the Lord is working among my tract people . . . O that I could see but one sinner constrained to come to Jesus."[16] Spurgeon was not "in the ministry"; he was a student and a school teacher who loved the Lord and wanted to use his free time to share the gospel with others.

Years later, when the pressures of ministry could easily take all of Spurgeon's time, he still made personal sharing of the gospel a priority. Faithful witnessing requires intention and planning. This is the great commission Jesus gave to His church (Matthew 28:19–20), and we must make it our great priority.

Never discount spiritual investments in the life of a child. When Spurgeon began preaching at sixteen years old, he already had a wealth of doctrinal knowledge and spiritual depth. Much of this was gleaned through the influence of his godly family and the books in his grandfather's library. His aunt who taught him to read, his parents and grandparents who surrounded him with spiritual influences, James Vinter who first encouraged his preaching . . . all of these and more had a part in the ministry of England's greatest preacher.

Is there a Charles Spurgeon among the children you encounter in your own life? You may never know, but no investment you make, especially spiritually, in the life of a child will ever be wasted. You may be making a difference for eternity.

God uses even unseen suffering to enlarge our ability to minister to others. Most people never saw the heavy seasons of depression Spurgeon wrestled through in private. But Spurgeon saw them as God's gift to enable him to better know "the God of all comfort; Who comforteth us in all our tribulation, that we may be able to comfort them which are in any trouble, by the comfort wherewith we ourselves are comforted of God" (2 Corinthians 1:3–4). He told his church family, "I would go to the deeps a hundred times to cheer a downcast spirit. It is good for me to have been afflicted, that I might know how to speak a word in season to one that is weary."[17]

Read good books, and study God's Word. Spurgeon read widely, sometimes as many as six books a week; and he had over ten thousand volumes in his personal library. His preaching evidenced his vast knowledge and retention of many of the great Puritan authors. But as much as Spurgeon read, he read Scripture even more. The advice he gave his students is good for us as well: "Visit many good books, but live in the Bible."[18]

The best way to answer a critic is to finish your task. Any great work for God will draw criticism. Spurgeon encountered heavy criticism throughout his entire ministry. But whether it was from a hostile press, jealous preachers, or even his own Pastor's College graduates, Spurgeon kept his hand to the plow and focused on the work in front of him which God had given him to do.

CONCLUSION

I s there a more thrilling chapter in Scripture than Hebrews 11? In thirty-one verses, the writer of Hebrews recounts the "faith moment" of ten Old Testament saints. Giving a couple verses each to these men and women, he briefly refers to their larger stories from the pages of the Old Testament.

But as he comes to the end of the chapter, he expresses what I feel now as we come to the end of this book: "And what shall I more say? for the time would fail me to tell of Gideon, and of Barak, and of Samson, and of Jephthae; of David also, and Samuel, and of the prophets" (Hebrews 11:32).

Indeed, there are so many more people we could study together—so many more men and women, outsiders, whose lives God has used to influence history.

Golgotha: The site where Jesus is believed to have been crucified lies just without the limits of the Old City of Jerusalem. It was by a major thoroughfare, and as He gave His life, "they that passed by reviled him, wagging their heads, And saying . . . If thou be the Son of God, come down from the cross" (Matthew 27:39–40).

But even in just these fifteen people whose lives we have barely glossed over, we come to the same conclusion as Hebrews 11: what these people did for God, they did "by faith."

By faith, they looked to Christ, stood for true doctrine, and labored for the gospel. And by faith, they made a difference for Christ.

There are, of course, many people who similarly labored by faith whose names we'll never know. Their sacrifices are not less honoring to their Lord or meaningful to His work.

For outsiders don't have "being known" as a goal—not even remotely. Neither do their goals include being respected or well thought of. The goal of an outsider is to live by faith and for Christ. It is to "go forth therefore unto him without the camp, bearing his reproach" (Hebrews 13:13).

The Garden Tomb: The power of the church does not rest in human effort or strategy. It is in "the working of his mighty power, Which he wrought in Christ, when he raised him from the dead . . ." (Ephesians 1:19–20).

If the furtherance of the gospel and the continuation of the church were up to human effort and strategy, we may very well come to the conclusion that to reach the world, we must accommodate the world. We might think that if we will embrace culture and soak in the philosophy of our day and adjust our doctrine to what is most palatable to those who do not yet know Christ, that we would be more likely to win converts.

But the furtherance of the gospel and the continuation of the church are not left to human strategy or power. In fact, we see through these fifteen lives that the church's greatest advances have come historically at its lowest ebb of opportunity.

It was during the persecution of the Waldensians that the gospel flourished. It was as England burned not only the Bibles Tyndale translated, but the preachers of those Bibles as well, that God's Word spread. It was as Manz preached and planted churches under the shadow of prison that the Anabaptists grew. It was as John Bunyan languished in prison that *Pilgrim's Progress* was written. And it was as the fires of persecution-driven revival diminished in England that God empowered the preaching of Charles Spurgeon.

When I look at the state of churches in America today and at the great needs around the world, I'm burdened. We need revival now more than we ever have before.

To carnal Christians, these statements probably sound extreme or alarmist. After all, Christianity still flourishes in America. We have conferences, books, podcasts, radio programs, and more resources for spiritual growth and gospel outreach than any generation before us.

But what we have too few of are outsiders.

There are many Christians who genuinely want to see the world reached with the gospel but believe that the way to do that is to compromise the faith or be nebulous in their convictions. Their church websites provide a weak statement of faith, if any. When asked about their beliefs on the moral issues of the day, they capitulate so as not to sound harsh or rejecting of others. Many churches and Christian institutions have experienced a drifting away from their mission and have seemingly blended back into the world they once tried to reach for Christ.

Where are the men and women willing to be outsiders for Christ?

Where are the Christians willing to sacrifice everything—including the respect and understanding of others . . . including their very lives—to remain true to Christ?

Where are the people who are willing to stand for Christ as the Apostle Paul, knowing it will mean a life described by the words in 1 Corinthians 4:12–13, ". . . being reviled, we bless; being persecuted, we suffer it: Being defamed, we intreat: we are made as the filth of the world, and are the offscouring of all things unto this day."

The world has enough Christians who fit into its mold.

But outsiders? There is plenty of room for more. There's always room "without the camp" with Jesus.

Will you come out? Will you be an outsider?

NOTES

Introduction

1. Alfred W. Light, *Bunhill Fields* (Stoke-on-Trent: Tentmaker Publications, 2003), 1.

2. Charles Haddon Spurgeon, *The Metropolitan Tabernacle Pulpit: Sermons, Parts 309–320* (London: Passmore & Alabaster, 1882), 249.

Chapter 1: Peter Waldo

1. John Foxe and George Townsend, *The Acts and Monuments of John Foxe, Volume 2* (London: Clay, Sons, and Taylor, 1870), 265.

2. Paul Thanasingh, *Peter Waldo and the Waldensian Movement* (Nashik, India: Eternal Light Books, 2017), Kindle Edition, locations 124–128.

3. Ibid., 173–175.

4. Foxe and Townsend, *The Acts and Monuments of John Foxe, Volume 2*, 265.

5. James A. Wylie, *The History of Protestantism, Volume 2* (London: Cassell, 1899), 486.

Chapter 2: John Wycliffe

1. Thomas Fuller, *The Church History of Britain, Volume 1* (London: Tegg, 1842), 493.

2. John Foxe and George Townsend, *The Acts and Monuments of John Foxe: With a Life of the Martyrologist, and Vindication of the Work, Volume 3* (London: Seeley, Burnside, and Seeley, 1844), 96.

Chapter 3: John Huss

1. J. Newton Brown, *Memorials of Baptist Martyrs* (Philadelphia: American Baptist Publication Society, 1854), 43.

2. Ken Curtis, "John Hus: Faithful unto Death," *Christianity*, April 28, 2010, https://www.christianity.com/church/church-history/timeline/1201-1500/john-hus-faithful-unto-death-11629878.html.

3. John Foxe, *Foxes Book of Martyrs*, rewritten and updated by Harold J. Chadwick (Gainsville, FL: Bridge-Logos, 2001), 84.

4. Ibid.

5. Ibid.

6. Ibid., 91.

7. Edythe Draper, *Draper's Book of Quotations for the Christian World* (Carol Stream, IL: Tyndale House, 1992), 628.

Chapter 4: Felix Manz

1. Erwin Lutzer, *Rescuing the Gospel: The Story and Significance of the Reformation* (Grand Rapids: BakerBooks, 2016), 156.

2. William R. Estep, *The Anabaptist Story* (Grand Rapids: William B. Eerdmans Publishing Company, 1975), 29.

3. Lutzer, *Rescuing the Gospel*, 158.

4. Estep, *The Anabaptist Story*, 31.

5. Ibid., 31–32.

6. J. Newton Brown, *Memorials of Baptist Martyrs* (Philadelphia: American Baptist Publication Society, 1854), 51.

7. Lutzer, *Rescuing the Gospel*, 158.

8. Estep, *The Anabaptist Story*, 29.

9. Lutzer, *Rescuing the Gospel*, 158.

Chapter 5: William Tyndale

1. Mark Galli, *131 Christians Everyone Should Know* (Nashville: B&H Publishing Group, 2000), 348–349. What Erasmus wrote was, "I totally disagree with those who are unwilling that the Holy Scriptures, translated into the common tongue, should be read by the unlearned. Christ desires his mysteries to be published abroad as widely as possible. . . . I would that [the Gospels and the epistles of Paul] were translated into all the languages, of all Christian people, that they might be read and known."

2. David Teems, *Tyndale: The Man Who Gave God an English Voice* (Nashville: Thomas Nelson, 2012), 39.

3. Brian H. Edwards, *God's Outlaw: The Story of William Tyndale* (Herts, England: Evangelical Press, 1976), 55–56.

4. John Foxe, *Foxes Book of Martyrs*, rewritten and updated by Harold J. Chadwick (Gainsville, FL: Bridge-Logos, 2001), 133.

5. David Daniell, *William Tyndale: A Biography* (New Haven: Yale University Press, 1994), 383.

6. S. L. Greenslade, *The Work of William Tindale* (London: Blackie & Son Limited, 1938), 23.

Chapter 6: Latimer and Ridley

1. John Foxe, *The Book of Martyrs*, condensed from the larger editions (London: Frederick Warne and Company, 1869), 181.

2. Allan Griffith Chester, *Hugh Latimer: Apostle to the English* (Philadelphia: University of Pennsylvania Press, 1954), 206.

3. Further complicating matters for Cranmer, he recanted after this sentencing. But instead of then being restored to the Catholic Church, as he had been promised, Mary insisted on his continued imprisonment. Cranmer, languishing in prison, grieved over his denial of truth and determined to restore his testimony. His moment came. Told that he would be allowed to make a public recantation of the earlier private ones, he was brought to the University Church. In reality, he was about to be executed, although he did not know this. He stood before the church, set aside the pre-written and pre-approved recantation, and preached. In his sermon, he renounced his recantations and boldly continued, "And as for the pope, I refuse him as Christ's enemy and Antichrist with all his false doctrine." That was as far as he got. He was led away to be burned in the same spot where Latimer and Ridley had died five months earlier.

4. Julius Lloyd, *History of the English Church, in Biographical Sketches* (London: Society for Promoting Christian Knowledge, 1879), 101.

5. Chester, *Hugh Latimer*, 216.

6. John Charles Ryle, *Light from Old Times, Or, Protestant Facts and Men* (London: Chas. J. Thynne, 1898), 158.

Chapter 7: Patrick Hamilton

1. Peter Lorimer, *Precursors of Knox: or, Memoires of Patrick Hamilton, Alexandre Alane, or Alesius, and Sir David Lindsay Collected from Original Sources: Vol. 1. Patrick Hamilton, the first Preacher and Martyr of the Scottish Reformation* (Edinburgh: Thomas Constable and Co., 1857), 152.

2. John Foxe, *Foxes Book of Martyrs*, rewritten and updated by Harold J. Chadwick (Gainsville, FL: Bridge-Logos, 2001), 109

3. Alexander F. Mitchell, *The Scottish Reformation: Its Epochs, Episodes, Leaders, and Distinctive Characteristics*, edited by David Hay Fleming (Edinburgh: William Blackwood and Sons, 1900), 35.

4. Tertullian, *Apologeticus*, (np: np, 197 AD), chapter 50.

Chapter 8: John Bunyan

1. John Bunyan, *Grace Abounding to the Chief of Sinners* (Aberdeen, Scotland: George King, 1840), 10.

2. Ibid., 17–18.

3. Ibid., 84–85.

4. John Brown, *John Bunyan: His Life, Times and Work* (London: The Hulbert Publishing Company, 1928), 105.

5. Ibid., 369.

6. Ray Comfort, *Spurgeon Gold* (Gainsville, FL: Bridge-Logos, 2005), 48.

7. Brown, *John Bunyan*, 224.

8. John Brown, *John Bunyan: His Life, Times and Work, Second Edition* (London: Wm. Isbister Limited, 1886), 158, paragraph breaks added.

9. Bunyan, *Grace Abounding to the Chief of Sinners*, 115.

10. John Piper, *The Hidden Smile of God: The Fruit of Affliction in the Lives of John Bunyan, William Cowper, and David Brainerd* (Wheaton, IL: Crossway Books, 2001), 57.

11. John Bunyan, *Israel's Hope Encouraged* in *The Works of John Bunyan, Vol. 1*, ed. George Offer (Edinburgh: The Banner of Truth Trust, 1991), 585.

Chapter 9: John Newton

1. D. Bruce Hindmarsh, *John Newton and the English Evangelical Tradition* (Grand Rapids: Eerdmans, 2001), 25.

2. William Cowper, *The Works of William Cowper: His Life, Letters, and Poems*, edited by T. S. Grimshawe (New York: Robert Carter and Brothers, 1851), 476.

3. John Piper, *The Hidden Smile of God: The Fruit of Affliction in the Lives of John Bunyan, William Cowper, and David Brainerd* (Wheaton, IL: Crossway Books, 2001), 110.

4. Gilbert Thomas, *William Cowper and the Eighteenth Century* (London: Ivor Nicholson and Watson, Ltd., 1935), 356.

5. John Piper, *The Roots of Endurance: Invincible Perseverance in the Lives of John Newton, Charles Simeon, and William Wilberforce* (Wheaton, IL: Crossway Books, 2002), 42.

6. William Budd Bodine, *Some Hymns and Hymn Writers Representing All who Profess and Call Themselves Christians* (Philadelphia: John C. Winston Company, 1907), 46.

7. John Newton, *Out of the Depths: The Autobiography of John Newton* (Kregel Publications, 1925, revised and updated by Dennis R. Hillman, 2003), 147.

8. Peter Rahme, *The Man and the Story Behind Amazing Grace* (Chullora, Australia: BC–AD, 2007).

9. F. M. Bladen, Alexander Britton, and James Cook, *Historical Records of New South*

Wales, Volume 2 (Sydney: Government Printer, 1892), Appendix A, 445, http://nla.gov.au/tarkine/nla.obj-359069774.

10. Jonathan Aitken, *John Newton: From Disgrace to Amazing Grace* (Crossway Books, 2007), 347.

Chapter 10: William Carey

1. Technically, a *cobbler* is only a shoe repairer, while a *cordwainer* is a shoemaker. As *cordwainer* has fallen out of common use, most people use *cobbler* to refer to either. Carey, however, who was aware of the limits of a cobbler, humbly referred to himself as such. As the story goes, someone trying to discredit his ideas regarding missions contemptuously said, "William Carey is just a maker of shoes." Carey interrupted to correct, "No, sir, I'm just a cobbler."

2. Dissenters were anyone not part of the Church of England, and although primarily Anabaptists/Baptists, dissenters included gospel-believing churches that didn't practice believer's baptism as well as Quakers, Separatists, and several cults.

3. F. Deauville Walker, *William Carey: Missionary Pioneer and Statesman* (Chicago: Moody Press, 1960), 47.

4. Timothy George, *Faithful Witness: The Life and Mission of William Carey* (Birmingham, Al.: New Hope, 1991), 19.

5. Eustace Carey, *Memoir of William Carey* (London: Jackson and Walford, 1836), 18.

6. This quote, often attributed to Carey, is actually a paraphrase from his book, *An Enquiry into the Obligations of Christians, to Use Means for the Conversion of the Heathens,* published in 1792. The full quote reads, "In order that the subject may be taken into more serious consideration, I shall enquire, whether the commission given by our Lord to his disciples be not still binding on us, take a short view

of former undertakings, give some account of the present state of the world, consider the practicability of doing something more than is done, and the duty of Christians in general in this matter."

7. I do not believe Calvinist doctrine, and although a thorough explanation is outside of the scope of this book, I would simply add a few thoughts here: Election in Scripture is specifically said to be based on God's foreknowledge not his predetermined will (1 Peter 1:2). Scripture repeatedly states that God's will is for all men to be saved (1 Timothy 2:4), that He allows men to choose against His will for their salvation (Romans 10:13), and that He has specifically commanded us to preach the gospel (Mark 16:15). He has even made the conversion of lost souls dependent on hearing the gospel preached (Romans 10:14).

8. Joseph Belcher, *William Carey: A Biography* (Philadelphia: American Baptist Publication Society, 1853), 19.

9. Eugene Myers Harrison, *Giants of the Missionary Trail* (Chicago: Scripture Press Foundation, 1954), 28.

10. Francis Augustus Cox, James Peggs, *History of the Baptist Missionary Society, from 1792 to 1842, Volume 1* (London: T. Ward & Company, and G. & J. Dyer, 1842), 20.

11. Harrison, *Giants of the Missionary Trail*, 31–32.

12. William Brown, *The History of Missions: Or, Of the Propagation of Christianity Among the Heathen, Since the Reformation, Volume 2* (Philadelphia: B. Coles, 1816), 212.

13. Carey, *Memoir of William Carey*, 457.

14. George, *Faithful Witness*, 16, emphasis added.

15. Vishal and Ruth Mangalwadi, *The Legacy of William Carey* (Wheaton, IL: Crossway Books, 1993, 1999), 62.

16. P. M. Stevenson, *William Carey* (Pasig City, Philippines: Life Line, nd), 95–96.

Chapter 11: George Müller

1. George Müller, *A Narrative of Some of the Lord's Dealings with George Müller, Volume 1* (London: J. Nisbet, 1837), 11.

2. Müller, *A Narrative of Some of the Lord's Dealings with George Müller, Volume 1*, 14–15.

3. George Müller, *A Narrative of Some of the Lord's Dealings with George Müller, Volume 2* (London: J. Nisbet, 1841), 110.

4. This story is relayed in *An Hour With George Müller: the Man of Faith to Whom God Gave Millions*, ed. A. Sims (Grand Rapids, Zondervan Publishing House, 1939), np.

5. Sims, *An Hour With George Müller*, np.

6. Roger Steer, *George Müller: Delighted in God!* (Wheaton, IL: Harold Shaw Publishers, 1981), 297.

7. Ibid.

8. Sims, *An Hour With George Müller*, np.

9. Ibid.

Chapter 12: Horatus Bonar

1. Horatius Bonar, *God's Way of Peace: A Book for the Anxious* (New York: Robert Carter & Brothers, 1878), 59–60.

2. Charles Seymour Robinson, *Annotations upon Popular Hymns* (New York: Hunt and Eaton, 1893), 223–224.

3. Norman Mable, *Popular Hymns and Their Writers* (London: Independent Press, Ltd., 1951), 44.

4. Jane Stuart Smith and Betty Carlson, *Great Christian Hymn Writers* (Wheaton, IL: Crossway Books, 1997), 40.

5. Ernest Edwin Ryden, *The Story of Our Hymns* (Rock Island, IL: Augustana Book Concern, 1930), 314.

6. *The Christian Treasury, Volume 24*, ed. Horatius Bonar, (Edinburgh: Johnstone, Hunter, and Co., 1868), 400.

Chapter 13: David Livingstone

1. Louise Seymour Houghton, *David Livingstone: The Story of One Who Followed Christ* (Philadelphia: Presbyterian Board of Publication, 1882), 17.

2. Ibid.

3. Houghton, *David Livingstone*, 45.

4. Galen B. Royer, *Christian Heroism in Heathen Lands* (Elgin, IL: Brethren Publishing House, 1917), 44.

5. George Seaver, *David Livingstone: His Life and Letters* (New York: Harper and Brothers, 1957), 186.

6. Ibid.

7. Eugene Myers Harrison, *Giants of the Missionary Trail* (Chicago: Scripture Press Foundation, 1954), 123–124.

8. Houghton, *David Livingstone*, 210–211.

9. Mark Galli, *131 Christians Everyone Should Know* (Nashville: B&H Publishing Group, 2000), 249.

10. Royer, *Christian Heroism in Heathen Lands*, 51.

11. Henry Morton Stanley, *How I Found Livingstone: Travels, Adventures, and Discoveries in Central Africa; Including Four Months' Residence with Dr. Livingstone, Volume 3* (Berlin: A. Asher and Co., 1873), 152.

12. William Garden Blaikie, *The Life of David Livingstone: Chiefly from His Unpublished Journals and Correspondence in the Possession of His Family* (London: John Murray, 1903), 190.

Chapter 14: Charles Spurgeon

1. G. Holden Pike, *James Archer Spurgeon* (np, np), 23.

2. Charles Haddon Spurgeon, *Spurgeon's Sermons Volume 11: 1865*, Anthony Uyl, ed. (Woodstock, Ontario: Devoted Publishing, 2017), 334.

3. Iain Murray, ed., *The Early Years* (London: Banner of Truth, 1962), 87–90.

4. Richard Day, *The Shadow of the Broad Brim: The Life and Legacy of Charles Haddon Spurgeon* (King of Prussia, PA: The Judson Press, 1934; Lancaster, CA: Striving Together Publications, 2013), 44.

5. Murray, *The Early Years*, 45.

6. C. H. Spurgeon, *The New Park Street and Metropolitan Tabernacle Pulpit, Volume 7* (London: Passmore and Alabaster, 1862), 225.

7. Murray, *The Early Years*, 193–194.

8. Ray Rhodes, *Susie: The Life and Legacy of Susannah Spurgeon* (Chicago: Moody Publishers, 2018), 50.

9. Ibid., 51.

10. Susannah Spurgeon and J. W. Harrald, *C. H. Spurgeon's Autobiography: 1854–1860* (London: Passmore and Alabaster, 1899), 192.

11. C. H. Spurgeon, *The Letters of Charles Haddon Spurgeon* (Collected and Collated by His Son Charles Spurgeon), (London: Marshall Brothers, Limited, 1923), 94, Logos Software.

12. "Charles H. Spurgeon," *Wholesome Words*, accessed March 12, 2019, https://www.wholesomewords.org/biography/biospurgeon6.html.

13. Charles Spurgeon, "Another Word Concerning the Down-Grade," *The Sword and the Trowel* (August 1887), 400.

14. Susannah Spurgeon and J. W. Harrald, *C. H. Spurgeon's Autobiography: 1878–1892* (London: Passmore and Alabaster, 1900), 255.

15. Arnold Dallimore, *C. H. Spurgeon: The New Biography* (Chicago: Moody Press, 1984), 239.

16. Iain Murray, ed., *The Early Years*, 46.

17. Susannah Spurgeon and J. W. Harrald, *C. H. Spurgeon's Autobiography: 1834–1854* (London: Passmore and Alabaster, 1899), 75.

18. "Leadership Quotes from Spurgeon – Part Two," *Lifeway*, accessed March 12, 2019, https://leadership.lifeway.com/2016/04/11/leadership-quotes-from-charles-spurgeon-part-two/.

Image Credits

Image on page 2 ©Alexander Hoernigk/CC BY-SA 4.0 (via Wikimedia Commons).

Image on page 34 is a reproduction of a painting that is in the public domain because of its age.

Images on pages 20, 122, 132, 142, 149, 151, and 158, courtesy of Monica Bass.

Image on page 196, public domain, obtained through the Gutenberg project.

Images on pages 236 and 237, courtesy of Larry Chappell.

Images on all other pages provided by the author.

ABOUT THE AUTHOR

D r. Paul Chappell is the senior pastor of Lancaster Baptist Church and the president of West Coast Baptist College in Lancaster, California. He is a powerful communicator of God's Word and a passionate servant to God's people. He has been married to his wife, Terrie, since 1980, and they have four married children who are all serving in Christian ministry. He enjoys spending time with his family and serving the Lord shoulder to shoulder with a wonderful church family.

Dr. Chappell's preaching is heard on Daily in the Word, a radio program that is broadcast across America. You can find a station listing at paulchappell.com/radio.

You can also connect with Dr. Chappell here:

Blog: paulchappell.com

Twitter: twitter.com/paulchappell

Facebook: facebook.com/pastor.paul.chappell

Other books by Paul Chappell...

ISBN: 978-1-59894-380-1

Paul Chappell's *Trust and Obey* devotional will encourage your spiritual growth. The readings conclude with a solid takeaway principle which you can apply to your life immediately. You'll be challenged and encouraged to follow Jesus more closely and to walk with Him in practical ways throughout each day.

STRIVINGTOGETHER.COM

ALSO AVAILABLE AS AN EBOOK

Other books by Paul Chappell...

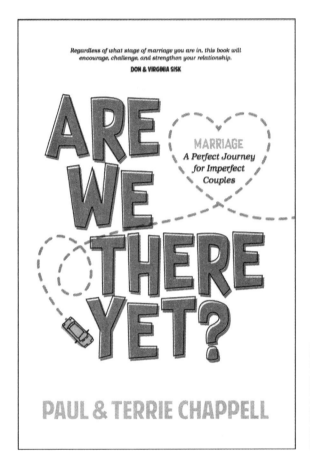

ISBN: 978-1-59894-353-5

This book is for every couple at any stage of the marriage journey. If you've lost your way...or lost your joy...or just want to get the most out of the journey, this book will help you clarify your destination and reveal a God-given perspective that can change and strengthen your marriage. A companion guide is sold separately.

STRIVINGTOGETHER.COM

ALSO AVAILABLE AS AN EBOOK

Other books by Paul Chappell...

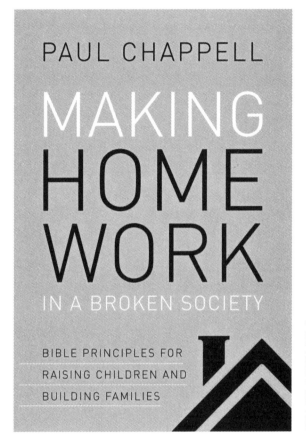

PAUL CHAPPELL

MAKING
HOME
WORK

IN A BROKEN SOCIETY

BIBLE PRINCIPLES FOR
RAISING CHILDREN AND
BUILDING FAMILIES

ISBN: 978-1-59894-310-8

Raising kids and building families is tough these days. God has
entrusted you, as a parent, to care for and raise your children
for Him—but it's not easy. Discover what it means to invest in
your children and how you can bring them up in the nurture and
admonition of the Lord.

STRIVINGTOGETHER.COM

ALSO AVAILABLE AS AN EBOOK